CONSUM

QUICK FIXES

Home
Improvement

pil Publications International, Ltd.

Walter Curtis is the author of numerous how-to books on home maintenance, repair, and remodeling. He also contributes articles to the Fix It Club (www.fixitclub.com).

Illustrator: Clarence A. Moberg

Interior photography: Dave Szarzak/White Eagle Studio

Louis Weber, CEO
Publications International, Ltd.
7373 North Cicero Avenue
Lincolnwood, Illinois 60712

Permission is never granted for commercial purposes.

ISBN-13: 978-1-4127-0438-0
ISBN-10: 1-4127-0438-3

Manufactured in USA

8 7 6 5 4 3 2 1

CONTENTS

HOME IMPROVEMENTS— THE QUICK AND EASY WAY!

Things break, with a little help or on their own. Light switches quit working. A window gets broken. A faucet leaks. And on and on. We all have a list of things we should fix if we had the time and know-how. Fortunately, most home repairs are really quick fixes.

ABOUT QUICK FIXES

A quick fix is a repair you can finish in a short time with basic tools and practically no prior experience. You don't have to be a plumber, for example, to fix a leaky faucet. You just need a little time plus a few tools and some clear instructions.

Finding the Time

The home improvements in this book are relatively easy to complete once you know what you're going to be doing and have gathered the needed parts and tools. (Don't worry, this book will show you how to find and choose them too.)

Working Smart

Here's the secret to quick fixes: Getting ready is half the job. Gathering the parts and tools and knowing what you need to do can be as time-consuming as actually making the repair. Fortunately, you can get ready for quick home improvements by simply reading this book and following the instructions. It may take you less time to do it than to read about it!

Getting Help

The first tip to keep in mind is never to throw away the owners manual that comes with any gadget. Instead, keep it in a place where you can find it easily. Manuals typically include troubleshooting and repair information, and they also usually tell you where to get parts and may even show you which parts to get. Using the make, model number, and part number, you can get a replacement part for virtually anything made in the past 10 years.

Find Parts When You Need Them

Where can you find replacement parts? For many quick fixes, parts are as near as your local hardware store. Each of the rows has signs to point you in the right direction: Paint, Wallcoverings, Fasteners, etc.

How can you be sure you are getting the correct part? If you've already removed the problem part, take it with you to the hardware store. If you don't have the broken part, find a knowledgeable clerk to help you. Or you can turn to nearby customers who look like they know what they're buying and ask for help.

That's another important tip: Ask for help. In fact, most clerks enjoy helping you get the right part. Just be sure the replacement part is the same as the old part.

What about hard-to-find parts? If you have access to the Internet, you can find one or more resources for just about any replacement part imaginable. Otherwise, check the telephone book for companies that sell the product you're fixing, call them, and ask about replacement parts.

Using This Book

Quick Fixes: Home Improvement is organized to help you get the most from your time and efforts. Before starting your first quick fix, read the section on tools, materials, and safety. You'll learn what tools you'll need for various home improvements as well as how to use them safely.

QUICK FIX TOOLS

Quick fixes means having the right tools and materials on hand so you can get at the job and on with your life. In this first section you'll learn to select and gather what you'll need for your toolbox to make the improvements featured in this book go smoothly.

What tools will you need? In the coming pages you'll learn about tools that measure, cut, drill, nail, tighten and loosen, hold, clamp, test, paint, and more. Most important, you'll learn which ones you really need and how to use them safely.

The first rule of tool safety is to buy good quality. High-quality tools are not only safer to use, but most will last a lifetime with proper care. It's also important to use your tools correctly. It may be tempting to use a screwdriver as a chisel, but doing so can damage the tool and, more important, damage you.

Never remove the safety guards installed on power equipment, and always wear safety goggles when working with power equipment. Please also note: The most dangerous tool is one that isn't well maintained. So, be diligent about tightening loose parts, fixing damaged cords, and sharpening dull blades.

Useful tools for your quick fix toolbox include measuring tools, drills, and fastener tools.

MEASURING AND MARKING TOOLS

Just about every home improvement project calls for accurate measurements. Not only do you have to know precisely how many feet and inches are involved, but you also need to ensure everything comes out plumb, level, and square. The following are basic devices for measuring and marking.

Tape Measure

Flexible tape measures are available in lengths of up to 50 feet; a tape that is 12 to 25 feet is usually adequate for most home improvement jobs. You should buy a tape at least ⅝ inch wide so it will stay rigid when extended.

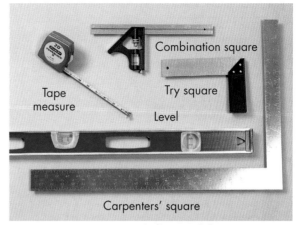

Common measuring tools for quick fixes

Square

The standard size for a carpenters' square is 18 to 24 inches (body) by 12 or 18 inches (tongue). The size is important for cutting straight edges on plywood and hardboard. For small jobs, a combination square is easier to use than a carpenters' square because the combination square is smaller—typically only 12 inches long. The square's body may incorporate a small bubble level or a scratch awl that can be used for leveling and marking. This type of square can also be used as a depth gauge, a miter square, and, with the blade removed, a straightedge and ruler.

Level

Two- and three-bubble levels are sufficient for most leveling needs. The edges of a level can be used as a straightedge. Laid flat against a vertical surface, a level can determine both horizontal and vertical levels. Levels are made of either wood or lightweight metal. Lengths range to 6 feet, with 30 inches being the most popular size.

Chalk Line

A chalk line is used for marking a straight line over long distances, such as for replacing wallpaper or flooring tiles.

Stud Finder

A stud finder comes in handy if you need to find the studs behind walls to hang a heavy item, for example.

HANDSAWS

Once measurements are made, materials can be cut using a saw. A wide selection of handsaws and power saws are available to match the needs of various cutting jobs.

Crosscut Saw

A crosscut saw, as its name implies, cuts across the grain of wood. A crosscut saw has five to ten or more teeth per inch to produce a smooth cut in the wood. It is used for cutting plywood and hardboard panels and for cutting miters (angles).

Ripsaw

A ripsaw cuts along the grain of wood, called "ripping." Its teeth are spaced three to five teeth per inch. Because a ripsaw's teeth are wider set than those of the crosscut saw, it can slice through wood like a chisel. The final cut of a ripsaw is rough, and the wood usually has to be sanded to its final measurement.

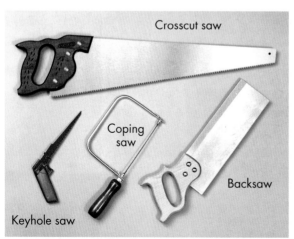

Common types of handsaws

Crosscut saw

Coping saw

Backsaw

Keyhole saw

Backsaw

A backsaw has a reinforced back to stiffen the blade. Its teeth are closely spaced—like those of a crosscut saw—so the cut is smooth. A backsaw is used for making angle cuts and for trimming molding. It's designed for use in a miter box; the reinforced back serves as a guide.

Keyhole Saw

A keyhole saw has a 10- to 12-inch tapered blade. It's used to cut openings for pipes, electrical boxes, and almost any straight or curved internal cuts that are too large for an auger bit, a drill, or a hole saw. A quality keyhole saw has removable blades with a variety of tooth spacings for cutting such materials as wood, plastic, metal, and hardboard.

Coping Saw

A coping saw has a thin blade that is secured with two pins at the ends of the saw. A variety of blades are available, with both ripsaw and crosscut tooth spacing.

Hacksaw

A hacksaw is used to cut metal, plastic, and pipe.

POWER SAWS

Power saws can be intimidating at first, and they should be! Improperly used, they can do damage in a hurry. You should always observe the proper safety precautions. Once you make a few practice cuts, however, you'll soon become comfortable with it.

Circular Saw

A portable electric tool, the circular saw is the power version of a crosscut saw or ripsaw. The guide on the saw can be adjusted to cut miters (angles) and pockets in most building materials. Several blades are available: crosscut, rip, masonry, metal, and plastic. A table is one of the accessories available for a circular saw so it can be mounted to work as a table saw.

Saber Saw

A saber saw, also called a jigsaw, consists of a 4-inch blade driven in an up-and-down or reciprocating motion. This portable power tool uses many blade designs for a variety of materials, including wood, metal, plastic, masonry, ceramic, and high-pressure laminate. This is the power counterpart to a keyhole and coping saw; it will make smooth fine-line or contour cuts either with or across the grain.

DRILLS

Three sizes of chuck to hold drill bits in place are available for power drills: ¼-inch, ⅜-inch, and ½-inch capacities. The two most popular sizes are ¼ and ⅜ inch. The ¼-inch chuck has a capacity of ¼-inch drills in metal and ½-inch drills in wood. A ¼-inch drill can handle only a limited range of drilling operations and shouldn't be used for difficult jobs, but it's the least expensive type of electric drill.

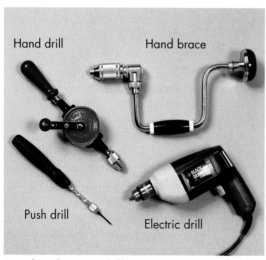

Hand drill

Hand brace

Push drill

Electric drill

Hand and power drills

The ⅜-inch drill can make ⅜-inch holes in metal and ¾-inch holes in wood; a hole saw can also be used with this tool to cut holes up to 3 inches in diameter. Many ⅜-inch drills have a hammer mode that permits drilling in concrete and a reversing feature that is handy for removing screws. A variable-speed drill is also a handy tool to own; the rotation can be started slowly and then sped up. A variety of attachments and accessories are available, including wire brushes, paint mixers, and even a circular saw attachment.

Power drills come in corded and cordless models. Cordless drills, which use an onboard battery and typically include a recharger, are becoming increasingly popular. The two main types of hand drills used are the push drill and the hand brace. Push drills are good for making pilot holes and for setting hinges. A hand brace is particularly handy when working in restricted areas because of its ratcheting head.

FASTENER TOOLS

Fastener tools are simply tools that help you apply fasteners. They include hammers, screwdrivers, wrenches, pliers, and clamps.

Hammers

The most popular hammer is the carpenters' curved-claw nail hammer; 16 ounces is a good size for men, 14 ounces for women. It is steel-headed; wood-, fiberglass-, or steel-handled; and used for driving nails and other fasteners. A flat-face, or plane-face, hammer is good for beginners to use, but it is more difficult to drive a nail flush to the work surface with this type of hammer.

Use a rubber mallet when you're trying to unstick windows or have to do light hammering on surfaces that can be damaged. Other specialty hammers include a ball-peen hammer for working with metal and a mason's hammer for brick and concrete projects.

Screwdrivers

Every toolbox should have one set of high-quality screwdrivers that are only used for tightening and loosening screws. There are many types of screwdrivers, which vary depending on the screw head each is designed to fit. The following are the most popular screw heads:

- **Standard head.** Also known as a flat, slotted, or straight screwdriver. Be sure the tip is the correct width and thickness to snugly fit the screw-head slot.

- **Phillips head.** Also called cross or X-head screwdrivers, Phillips heads fit into a cross-shape recess in the screw or bolt head.

- **Torx head.** Torx head (or similar designs called Robertson) screwdrivers fit into a square or hexagonal hole, which allows more torque for tightening or loosening the fastener.

Wrenches

The purpose of a wrench is to turn a bolt head or nut. Selecting the appropriate wrench depends on the fastener's design and size. It can also depend on how difficult the fastener is to reach. Wrench types include open end, combination, adjustable, and Allen. **Tip:** When using a wrench, pull it toward you rather than pushing it away to give you more control.

- **Closed end.** A closed, or box, end wrench is used where there is room to place the wrench mouth around the fastener. Closed end wrenches are available in 6- and 12-point versions to match the number of sides on the fastener. Hexagon fasteners have 6 sides, or points, and are the most popular.

- **Open end.** This type of wrench is used for turning fasteners in locations where a box end wrench cannot encompass the fastener.

- **Combination.** A combination wrench has ends that perform specific tasks. One end may be open and the other closed, one may be offset and the other straight, or the two ends might be of fractionally different sizes.

- **Adjustable.** An adjustable wrench can be used on various fastener sizes. The disadvantage is that it is less stable than a fixed-size wrench and can easily injure you or damage the fastener. It should be used only if the correct size wrench is not available.

- **Socket.** Socket wrenches fit over the fastener, making removal easier and safer than with other wrenches. Sockets come in standard and extended depth; extensions are available. They are often purchased in sets by drive size.

- **Allen.** Called by the Allen brand name, these are used on fasteners with a hexagonal hole in the head. Allen wrenches are available with L- or T-shape handles.

Pliers

Pliers are used to grasp and hold a part. They should not be used as wrenches to tighten or loosen fasteners. Common types of pliers include slip-joint, groove-joint, needle-nose, and locking.

- **Slip-joint.** This type of pliers has two settings in the handle to allow for two widths. Once the correct width is selected, the handles are closed together to force the jaw around the part and hold it securely.

- **Groove-joint.** Groove-joint pliers are similar to slip-joint except they use an elongated hole in the handle with grooves that allow multiple widths.

- **Needle-nose.** This type has jaws that come to a point for securely grasping small parts or wires, especially in tight locations.

- **Locking.** Sometimes called by the Vise Grip brand name, locking pliers are adjustable and can be locked to hold a part in place.

Clamps

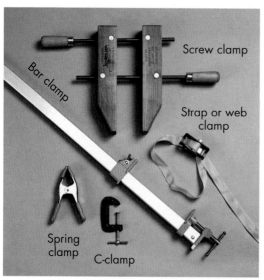

Various types of clamps

Clamps are essential for some quick fixes, like holding parts together while glue dries. Spring clamps, which look like large metal clothespins, are inexpensive and are used for clamping small jobs, such as gluing veneers to core material. C-clamps are also useful and come in a wide range of sizes. They are made from cast iron or aluminum and have a C-shape body. A screw with a metal pad applies tension on the material being clamped. Because C-clamps can exert a lot of pressure, buffer blocks of scrap wood should be inserted between the jaws of the clamps and the material being clamped. Screw, bar, and strap clamps are used by woodworkers.

PAINTING TOOLS

A good paint job depends as much on selecting the right tools as on selecting the right paint. With the proper equipment, even inexperienced do-it-yourselfers can do a professional-quality job.

Paintbrushes

With few exceptions, paintbrushes fall into two camps: natural bristle brushes, made of animal hair, and synthetic bristle brushes, usually made of nylon. The naturals were once considered the best, but today the synthetics are every bit as good.

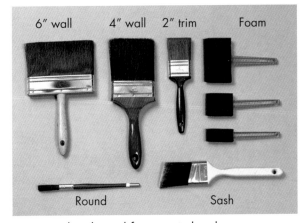

Common bristle and foam paintbrushes

Regardless of price, you can distinguish between a good brush and a bad one by examining them closely at the store. Spread the bristles and inspect the tips. The more flags, or split ends, the better the brush and its paint-spreading capabilities. Rap the brush on the edge of a counter; a good brush may lose a few bristles, but a bad one will lose many. Find a brush with long, tapered bristles, particularly on narrow brushes. As a general rule, the bristle length should be about one-and-a-half times as long as the width of the brush (the exception is with wider brushes, often called wall brushes). Finally, choose smooth, well-shaped handles of wood or plastic that comfortably fit in your hand.

Paintbrushes come in a wide variety of sizes and types and are necessary for those hard-to-reach spots a paint roller can't reach. Here are some of the main types of paintbrushes:

- **Wall.** This type spreads the most paint over the most surface. A 4-inch-wide brush is a good choice.

- **Trim.** A 2-inch-wide trim brush is ideal for woodwork and for "cutting in" around windows, doors, and corners.

- **Sash.** Available in 1-, 1½-, or 2-inch widths, the angled sash brush makes close work easier. Used carefully, it reduces the need to use tape to protect windowpanes.

The same size brushes are also available in foamed urethane. These disposable foam brushes are increasingly popular among do-it-yourselfers. They come in widths up to 3 inches and are inexpensive enough to toss out after one use.

Paint Rollers

For large, flat surface areas like walls and ceilings, paint rollers will help you get the job done in about half the amount of time it would take with a paintbrush. Most painters use brushes for trim work and around windows and doors, then turn to rollers to fill in the big blank spaces. Rollers for painting flat areas come in varying widths—from 4 to 18 inches—but the two most common sizes for interior jobs are 7 inches and 9 inches wide.

Paint rollers intended for wall or ceiling painting have handles made of plastic or wood that may have been hollowed out and machined to accept an extension handle. They also have a metal or plastic frame that is slipped inside a roller cover. Of the two types, the metal-rib version (also known as a birdcage or spring-metal frame) is best because it's easier to clean and less likely to stick to the inside of the roller cover.

The type of roller cover you should buy is largely determined by the kind of paint you'll be using, but they are all fiber-covered or urethane-foam-covered cylinders that soak up paint from a tray and

Paint rollers, pad, and tray

then release it when rolled over a flat surface. The rolling action creates a vacuum that actually pulls the paint off the roller. Made of lamb's wool, mohair, Dynel, acetate, or polyurethane foam, most rollers are labeled with the kind of paint for which they are intended to be used. Choose your roller cover accordingly. The roller package will also identify the length of the roller cover's nap, or pile, which can vary from $\frac{1}{16}$ inch to $1\frac{1}{2}$ inches. For rough surfaces, use the long naps; choose short ones for smooth surfaces. The pile is attached to a tube that slips over the roller's plastic or cardboard frame.

Paint trays are made of aluminum or plastic and come in standard 7-inch and 9-inch versions. The 9-inch size is most popular because you can then use either a 7- or 9-inch roller. Some trays come with hooks that allow you to attach them directly to a ladder. The trays, of course, are washable and durable. But to make cleanup even easier, it's best to buy some disposable plastic tray liners or line the tray with aluminum foil.

OTHER QUICK FIX TOOLS

Planes

Need to shave the edge of a sticking door? Use a jack plane to remove excess wood and bring the surface of the wood to trueness and smoothness; a smoothing plane brings wood to a final finish. A block plane can do both, plus it is used to smooth and cut the end grain of wood. All are relatively inexpensive and can be found at most hardware stores.

Electric Sander

Need to sand a surface but don't have all day? An orbital sander is the handiest for most small projects.

QUICK FIX MATERIALS

To make a quick fix you need to know what materials to select and how to use them. This section offers basic information on selecting lumber, plywood, drywall, and other materials for common do-it-yourself projects.

LUMBER

Maybe you've noticed that lumber sizes are often misleading. The "nominal" cross-section dimensions of a piece of lumber, such as 2×4 or 1×6, are always somewhat larger than the actual, or dressed, dimensions. The reason is that dressed lumber has been surfaced or planed smooth on four sides (called S4S). The nominal measurement is made before the lumber is surfaced.

Board measure is a method of measuring lumber in which the basic unit is 1 foot long by 1 foot wide by 1 inch thick, called a board foot. It is calculated by nominal, not actual, dimensions of lumber. The easiest formula for figuring nominal board feet is:

$$\frac{\text{Thickness} \times \text{Width} \times \text{Length}}{12}$$

The answer is in board feet. Lumber is often priced in board feet. However, most building material retailers and lumberyards also price lumber by the running foot for easier calculation. That is, a 2×4×8 is priced at eight times the running foot cost rather than as 5.333 board feet.

PLYWOOD

Some quick fixes require that you use or at least understand plywood. Knowing about plywood can save you money and may mean the difference between a successful project and one that fails. For example, you don't need to buy an expensive piece of plywood that's perfect on both sides if only one side will be seen. Similarly, there's no sense in paying for ⅝-inch thickness when ¼-inch plywood is really all you need. Plywood also comes with different glues, veneers, and degrees of finish. By knowing these characteristics you may be able to save money as well as do a better job.

One-by (1×) lumber is called board:

Nominal Size	Dressed Dimensions (inches)
1×6	¾×5½
1×8	¾×7¼
1×10	¾×9¼

Two-by (2×) and four-by (4×) lumber is called dimension lumber:

Nominal Size	Dressed Dimensions (inches)
2×2	1½×1½
2×4	1½×3½
2×6	1½×5½
2×8	1½×7¼
2×10	1½×9¼
2×12	1½×11¼
4×4	3½×3½

Available at home centers, hardware stores, and lumberyards, plywood is better than lumber for some jobs. It is strong, lightweight, and rigid. Its high-impact resistance means plywood doesn't split, chip, crack all the way through, or crumble; the cross-laminate construction restricts expansion and contraction within the individual plies. Moreover, you never get "green" wood with plywood. When you buy a sheet of plywood, you know exactly what size you're getting, unlike with other types of lumber that have nominal and actual measurements. For example, a 4×8-foot sheet of ¾-inch plywood measures exactly 4 by 8 feet and is exactly ¾ inch thick.

Plywood is broadly categorized into two types: exterior and interior. Exterior plywood is made with nothing but waterproof glue and should always be used for any exposed application. Interior plywood, made with highly resistant glues, can actually withstand quite a bit of moisture. There is interior plywood made with IMG (intermediate glue), which is resistant to bacteria, mold, and moisture, but no interior plywood is made for use outdoors.

When purchasing plywood, look for a back stamp or edge marking bearing the initials APA or DFPA. APA stands for American Plywood Association, while DFPA is the Douglas Fir Plywood Association. These two organizations represent most of the plywood manufacturers, and they inspect and test all plywood to ensure quality is high and grading is accurate. The most critical plywood-grading category for most home projects is the appearance grade of the panel faces.

An increasingly popular substitute for plywood is oriented strand board (OSB), or waverboard, made from compressed wood chips held together with glue. Your lumber supplier will have it near the plywood products.

DRYWALL

Quick fixes to drywall typically mean patching drywall rather than replacing it. However, you should know something about drywall before you tackle a repair. Drywall, also known as gypsum wallboard, has all but replaced plaster in modern homes. Its rocklike gypsum core makes drywall as fire-resistant as plaster, and its heavy paper facing eliminates the cracking problems that plague plaster walls. Best of all, drywall is far easier to work with than plaster.

The standard-size sheets for walls measure 4×8 feet. All drywall sheets are 4 feet wide, but many building material outlets offer 10-foot and even 12-foot lengths. The most popular thicknesses of drywall are ½ inch (typically for walls) and ⅝ inch (ceilings).

QUICK FIX FASTENERS

Most home improvement projects require fasteners such as nails, screws, glues, and bolts. The following are some of the most common types of fasteners and advice on how to select the right one for your quick fix.

NAILS

Most commonly, nails are made of steel, but other types—aluminum, brass, nickel, bronze, copper, and stainless steel—are available for use where corrosion could occur. In addition, nails are manufactured with coatings—galvanized, blued, or cemented—to prevent rusting and to increase their holding power.

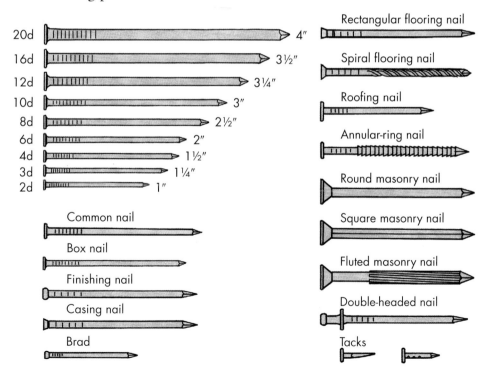

Nail penny sizes

Nail size is designated by penny size, originally the price per hundred nails. Penny size, almost always referred to as "d," ranges from 2 penny, or 2d (1 inch long), to 60 penny, or 60d (6 inches long). Nails shorter than 1 inch are called brads; nails longer than 6 inches are called spikes.

The length of the nail is important, because at least two-thirds of the nail should be driven into the base, or thicker, material. For example, a 1×3 nailed to a 4×4 beam should be fastened with an 8 penny, or 8d, nail. An 8d nail is 2½ inches long; ¾ inch of its length will go through the 1×3, and the remaining 1¾ inches will go into the beam. What follows are some of the most popular nail types.

Common Nails

Used for most medium to heavy construction work, this type of nail has a thick head and can be driven into tough materials. Common nails are made from wire and cut to the proper length and are available in sizes 2d through 60d.

Box Nails

Lighter and smaller in diameter than common nails, box nails are designed for light construction and household use.

Finishing Nails

Finishing nails are lighter than common nails and have a small head. They are often used for installing paneling and trim where you do not want the nail head to show.

Roofing Nails

Usually galvanized, roofing nails have a much larger head than common nails. This helps to prevent damage to asphalt shingles.

Drywall Nails

Nails made for drywall installation are often ringed and have an indented head. Annular-ring nails have sharp ridges all along the nail shaft, providing greater holding power.

Masonry Nails

There are three types of masonry nails designed for use with concrete and concrete block: round, square, and fluted. Masonry nails should not be used where high strength is required. Fastening to brick, stone, or reinforced concrete should be made with screws or lag bolts.

Tacks

Available in both round and cut forms, tacks are used to hold carpet or fabric to wood. Upholstery tacks often have decorative heads.

Corrugated Fasteners

Corrugated fasteners, also called wiggly nails, are used for light-duty joints where strength is not important. The fasteners are set at right angles to the joint.

SCREWS

Screws provide more strength and holding power than nails. Additionally, if something needs to be disassembled, screws can easily be removed. Like nails, screws are available with different coatings to deter rust. They are manufactured with four basic heads and different kinds of slots. Flathead screws are almost always countersunk into the material being fastened so the head of the screw is flush with (or lower than) the surface. Ovalhead screws are partially countersunk, with about half the screw head above the surface. Roundhead screws are not countersunk; the entire screw head lies above the surface. Fillister-head screws are raised above the surface on a flat base to keep the screwdriver from damaging the surface as the screw is tightened.

Most screws have slot heads and are driven with slotted, or standard, screwdrivers. Phillips-head screws have crossed slots and are driven with Phillips screwdrivers. Screws are measured in both length and diameter at the shank, which is designated by gauge number from 0 to 24. Length is measured in inches. The length of a screw is important because at least half the length of the screw should extend into the base material. **Tip:** To prevent screws from splitting the material, pilot holes must be made with a drill before the screws are driven.

For most home repair purposes, wood screws will suffice. Sheet metal screws, machine screws, and lag screws also come in various types. If you're trying to replace one of these screws, take an old screw with you to the hardware store.

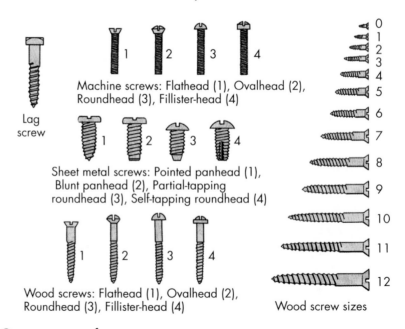

Lag screw

Machine screws: Flathead (1), Ovalhead (2), Roundhead (3), Fillister-head (4)

Sheet metal screws: Pointed panhead (1), Blunt panhead (2), Partial-tapping roundhead (3), Self-tapping roundhead (4)

Wood screws: Flathead (1), Ovalhead (2), Roundhead (3), Fillister-head (4)

Wood screw sizes

Common types of screws

Wood Screws

Wood screws are usually made of steel, although brass, nickel, bronze, and copper screws should be used if there is potential for corrosion.

Sheet Metal Screws

Use this type of screw to fasten pieces of metal together. Sheet metal screws form threads in the metal as they are installed. There are several different types of sheet metal screws. Pointed panhead screws are coarse-threaded; they are available in gauges from 4 to 14 and lengths from ¼ inch to 2 inches. Pointed panheads are used in light sheet metal. Blunt panhead screws are used for heavier sheet metal; they are available in gauges from 4 to 14 and lengths from ¼ inch to 2 inches. Both types of panhead screws are available with either plain or Phillips-head slots.

Roundhead Screws

Partial-tapping roundhead screws have finer threads; they can be used in soft or hard metals. They are available in diameters from ³⁄₁₆ inch to 1¼ inches. Self-tapping roundhead screws are used for heavy-duty work with thick sheet metal and are available in diameters from ¼ inch to 2 inches and in lengths from ⅛ to ¾ inch. Both types of roundhead screws are available with either plain or Phillips-head slots.

Machine Screws

Machine screws are blunt-ended screws used to fasten metal parts together. They are commonly made of steel or brass. Like other fasteners, they are also made with coatings— brass, copper, nickel, zinc, cadmium, and galvanized—that help deter rust. Machine screws are manufactured with each

DRILLING FOR WOOD SCREWS

Gauge Number	Decimal Diameter	Fractional Diameter	Shank Hole Twist Bit	Shank Hole Drill Gauge	Pilot Hole Hardwood Twist Bit s	Hardwood Twist Bit p	Hardwood Drill Gauge s	Hardwood Drill Gauge p	Softwood Twist Bit s	Softwood Twist Bit p	Softwood Drill Gauge s	Softwood Drill Gauge p	Auger Bit Number	Threads per Inch
0	.060	1/16–	1/16	52	1/32	–	70	–	1/64	–	75	–	–	32
1	.073	5/64–	5/64	47	1/32	–	66	–	1/32	–	71	–	–	28
2	.086	5/64+	3/32	42	3/64	1/32	56	70	1/32	1/64	65	75	3	26
3	.099	3/32+	7/64	37	1/16	1/32	54	66	3/64	1/32	58	71	4	24
4	.112	6/64+	7/64	32	1/16	3/64	52	56	3/64	1/32	55	65	4	22
5	.125	1/8–	1/8	30	5/64	1/16	49	54	1/16	3/64	53	58	4	20
6	.138	9/64–	9/64	27	5/64	1/16	47	52	1/16	3/64	52	55	5	18
7	.151	5/32–	5/32	22	3/32	5/64	44	49	1/16	3/64	51	53	5	16
8	.164	5/32+	11/64	18	3/32	5/64	40	47	5/64	1/16	48	52	6	15
9	.177	11/64+	3/16	14	7/64	3/32	37	44	5/64	1/16	45	51	6	14
10	.190	3/16+	3/16	10	7/64	3/32	33	40	3/32	5/64	43	48	6	13
11	.203	13/64–	13/64	4	1/8	7/64	31	37	3/32	5/64	40	45	7	12
12	.216	7/32–	7/32	2	1/8	7/64	30	33	7/64	3/32	38	43	7	11
14	.242	15/64+	1/4	D	9/64	1/8	25	31	7/64	3/32	32	40	8	10
16	.268	17/64+	17/64	I	5/32	1/8	18	30	9/64	7/64	29	38	9	9
18	.294	19/64–	19/64	N	3/16	9/64	13	25	9/64	7/64	26	32	10	8
20	.320	21/64–	21/64	P	13/64	5/32	4	18	11/64	9/64	19	29	11	8
24	.372	3/8	3/8	V	7/32	3/16	1	13	3/16	9/64	15	26	12	7

s = Slotted head   p = Phillips head

of the four basic types of heads—flathead, ovalhead, round-head, and fillister-head—and with both plain and Phillips-head slots. They are typically available in gauges 2 to 12, diameters from 1/4 inch to 1/2 inch, and lengths from 1/4 inch to 3 inches.

Lag Screws

For light work, lead, plastic, or fiber plugs (called anchors) can be used to hold screws. But for larger jobs and more holding power, lead expansion anchors and lag screws are used. Lag screws are heavy-duty fasteners. They are driven with a wrench and are used primarily for fastening to masonry or wood framing. The anchors are inserted into holes drilled in the masonry, and the lag screws are driven firmly into the anchors.

BOLTS

Bolts are used with nuts and often with washers. The three basic types are carriage bolts, stove bolts, and machine bolts. Other types include the masonry bolt and anchor, toggle bolt, and expansion bolt, which are used to distribute weight when fastening something to a hollow wall. Machine bolts are manufactured in two gauges: fine-threaded and coarse. Carriage and stove bolts are coarse-threaded. Bolt size is measured by shank diameter and by threads per inch, expressed as diameter by threads (for example, $\frac{1}{4} \times 20$). Carriage bolts are available up to 10 inches long, stove bolts up to 6 inches, and machine bolts up to 30 inches. Larger sizes usually must be special ordered.

Carriage Bolts

Carriage bolts are used mainly in making furniture. They have a round head with a square collar and are tightened into place with a nut and wrench. The collar fits into a prebored hole or twists into the wood, preventing the bolt from turning as the nut is tightened. Carriage bolts are coarse-threaded and are available in diameters from $\frac{3}{16}$ to $\frac{3}{4}$ inch and lengths from $\frac{1}{2}$ inch to 10 inches.

Stove Bolts

Stove bolts aren't just for stoves; they are quite versatile and can be used for almost any fastening job. They are available in a wide range of sizes, have a slotted head—flat, oval, or round, like screws—and are driven with a screwdriver or tightened into place with a nut and wrench. Most stove bolts are completely threaded, but the larger ones may have a smooth shank near the bolt head. Stove bolts are coarse-threaded and are available in diameters from $5/32$ to $1/2$ inch and lengths from $3/8$ inch to 6 inches.

Machine Bolts

Machine bolts have either a square head or a hexagonal head. They are fastened with square nuts or hex nuts and are wrench-driven. Machine bolts are manufactured in very large sizes; the bolt diameter increases with length. They are either coarse-threaded or fine-threaded and are available in diameters from $1/4$ inch to 2 inches and lengths from $1/2$ inch to 30 inches.

Masonry Bolts and Anchors

These work on the same principle as the lag bolt or screw; a plastic sleeve expands inside a predrilled hole as the bolt is tightened.

Hollow Wall Bolts

Toggle bolts and expansion bolts are used for fastening lightweight objects, such as picture frames, to hollow walls. Toggle bolt wings are opened inside the wall by a spring. Expansion bolts are inserted into an expansion jacket, which expands as the bolt is tightened. The bolts are available in diameters from $1/8$ to $1/2$ inch and lengths up to 8 inches for walls as thick as $1 3/4$ inches.

ADHESIVES

Adhesives chemically attach two or more surfaces together. The right adhesive can make any fix quicker and longer lasting. Here's some information on adhesives frequently used by do-it-yourselfers.

Multipurpose Adhesives

If you keep a small assortment of multipurpose adhesives in stock you will be able to make a wide variety of repairs. The following are the most common types of multipurpose adhesives.

- **White glue** (polyvinyl acetate, or PVA). PVA glue is a white liquid, usually sold in plastic bottles. It is recommended for use on porous materials—wood, paper, cloth, porous pottery, and nonstructural wood-to-wood bonds. It is not water-resistant. Clamping is required for 30 minutes to 1 hour to set the glue; curing time is 18 to 24 hours. School glue, a type of white glue, dries more slowly. Inexpensive and nonflammable, PVA glue dries clear.

- **Epoxy.** Epoxies are sold in tubes or in cans. They consist of two parts—resin and hardener—that must be thoroughly mixed just before use. They are very strong, very durable, and very water-resistant. Epoxies are recommended for use on metal, ceramics, some plastics, and rubber; they aren't recommended for flexible surfaces. Clamping is required for about 2 hours for most epoxies. Drying time is about 12 hours; curing time is one to two days. Epoxy dries clear or amber and is more expensive than other adhesives.

- **Cyanoacrylate.** Also called super or instant glue, cyanoacrylate is similar to epoxy but is a one-part glue. These glues form a very strong bond and are recommended for use on materials such as metal, ceramics, glass, some plastics, and rubber; they aren't recommended for flexible surfaces. Apply sparingly. Clamping is not required; curing time is one to two days. Cyanoacrylates dry clear.

- **Contact cement.** A rubber-base liquid sold in bottles and cans, contact cement is recommended for bonding laminates, veneers, and other large areas and for repairs. It can also be used on paper, leather, cloth, rubber, metal, glass, and some plastics because it remains flexible when it dries. It is not recommended for repairs where strength is necessary. Contact cement should be applied to both surfaces and allowed to set; the surfaces are then pressed together for an instant bond. No repositioning is possible once contact has been made. Clamping isn't required; curing is complete on drying. Contact cement is usually very flammable.

- **Polyurethane glue.** This high-strength glue is an amber paste and is sold in tubes. It forms a very strong bond similar to that of epoxy. Polyurethane glue is recommended for use on wood, metal, ceramics, glass, most plastics, and fiberglass. It dries flexible and can also be used on leather, cloth, rubber, and vinyl. Clamping is required for about 2 hours; curing time is about 24 hours. Polyurethane glue dries translucent and can be painted or stained. Its shelf life is short, and it is expensive.

- **Silicone rubber adhesive or sealant.** Silicone rubber glues and sealants are sold in tubes and are similar to silicone rubber caulk. They form very strong, very durable waterproof bonds, with excellent resistance to high and low temperatures. They're recommended for use on gutters and on building materials, including metal, glass, fiberglass, rubber, and wood. They can also be used on fabrics, some plastics, and ceramics. Clamping is usually not required; curing time is about 24 hours, but the adhesive skins over in less than 1 hour. Silicone rubber adhesives dry flexible and are available in clear, black, and metal colors.

- **Household cement.** The various adhesives sold in tubes as household cement are fast-setting, low-strength glues.

Recommended for use on wood, ceramics, glass, paper, and some plastics, some household cements dry flexible and can be used on fabric, leather, and vinyl. Clamping is usually not required; setting time is 10 to 20 minutes, curing time is up to 24 hours.

- **Hot-melt adhesive.** Hot-melt glues are in stick form and used with glue guns. A glue gun heats the adhesive above 200°F. For the best bond, the surfaces to be joined should be preheated. Because hot-melt adhesives are only moderately strong and bonds will come apart if exposed to high temperatures, this type of glue is recommended for temporary bonds of wood, metal, paper, and some plastics and composition materials. Clamping isn't required; setting time is 10 to 45 seconds, and curing time is 24 hours.

Wood Glues

Wood glues are specifically made for wood repair projects. Here are your main choices:

- **Yellow glue** (aliphatic resin or carpenters' glue). Aliphatic resin glue is a yellow liquid, usually sold in plastic squeeze bottles and often labeled as carpenters' glue. Yellow glue is very similar to white glue but forms a slightly stronger bond. It is also a bit more water-resistant than white glue. Clamping is required for about 30 minutes until the glue sets; curing time is 12 to 18 hours. Yellow glue dries clear but does not accept wood stains.

- **Plastic resin glue** (urea formaldehyde). Plastic resin glue is recommended for laminating layers of wood and for gluing structural joints. It is water-resistant but not waterproof and isn't recommended for use on outdoor furniture. This glue is resistant to paint and lacquer thinners. Clamping is required for up to 8 hours; curing time is 18 to 24 hours.

- **Resorcinol glue**. This glue is waterproof and forms strong and durable bonds. It is recommended for use on outdoor furniture, kitchen counters, structural bonding, boats, and sporting gear. It can also be used on concrete, cork, fabrics, leather, and some plastics. Resorcinol glue has excellent resistance to temperature extremes, chemicals, and fungus. Clamping is required; curing time is 8 to 24 hours, depending on humidity and temperature.

Adhesives for Glass and Ceramics

Most multipurpose adhesives will bond glass and ceramics, but specialized versions often bond them more securely.

- **China and glass cement.** Many cements are sold for mending china and glass. These cements usually come in tubes. Acrylic latex-base cements have good resistance to water and heat. Clamping is usually required.

- **Silicone rubber adhesives.** Only silicone adhesives made specifically for glass and china are recommended. They form very strong bonds, with excellent resistance to water and temperature extremes. Clamping is usually required.

Metal Adhesives and Fillers

Need to make a repair in metal? Here are some popular adhesives that can make a strong bond with metal:

- **Steel epoxy.** A two-part compound sold in tubes, steel epoxy is quite similar to regular epoxy. It forms a very strong, durable, heat- and water-resistant bond and is recommended for patching gutters and gas tanks, sealing pipes, and filling rust holes. Drying time is about 12 hours; curing time is 24 to 48 hours.

- **Steel putty.** This putty consists of two putty-consistency parts that are kneaded together before use. It forms a strong, water-resistant bond and is recommended for patching and sealing pipes that aren't under pressure. It can also be used for ceramic and masonry. Curing time is about 30 minutes; when dry, it can be sanded or painted.

- **Plastic metal cement.** Plastic metal is one-part adhesive and filler. It is moisture-resistant but cannot withstand temperature extremes. This type of adhesive is recommended for use on metal, glass, concrete, and wood, where strength is not required. Curing time is about four hours; when dry, plastic metal cement can be sanded or painted.

Plastic Adhesives

Plastics present a special problem with some adhesives because solvents in the adhesives can dissolve plastic. Here are some popular plastic adhesives:

- **Model cement.** Usually sold in tubes as "model maker" glues, model cement forms a strong bond on acrylics and polystyrenes and can be used on most plastics, except plastic foam. Clamping is usually required until the cement has set (about 10 minutes); curing time is about 24 hours. Model cement dries clear.

- **Vinyl adhesive.** Vinyl adhesives, sold in tubes, form a strong, waterproof bond on vinyl and on many plastics, but don't use them on plastic foam. Clamping is usually not required. Vinyl adhesive dries flexible and clear; curing time is 10 to 20 minutes.

- **Acrylic solvent.** Solvents are not adhesives as such; they act by melting the acrylic bonding surfaces, fusing them together at the joint. They are recommended for use on acrylics and polycarbonates. Clamping is required; the bonding surfaces are clamped or taped together, and the solvent is injected into the joint with a syringe. Setting time is about five minutes.

OTHER QUICK FIX SUPPLIES

As you tackle the home improvement projects in this book you'll need other supplies, such as paint and abrasives. Let's first take a look at the various paints available.

INTERIOR PAINTS

Although paints are available for every possible surface, there is no such thing as an all-surface paint. The wrong paint can damage a surface and often not adhere well, so it's crucial to know in advance what goes where and when. Fortunately, modern paint technology has taken a lot of the risk out of choosing the proper paint. Formulas for "latex paints," for example, have been improved to withstand dirt, moisture, and daily wear and tear, so these paints are no longer reserved exclusively for low-traffic areas. They are as washable and durable as the old oilbase paints.

Still, an important factor in paint selection is gloss. Regardless of the type of coating you choose, the gloss of the one you buy will affect both its appearance and its durability. High-gloss paints are the most durable because they contain more resin than either semigloss or flat paints. Resin is an ingredient that hardens as the paint dries. The more resin, the harder the surface. Consequently, for kitchens, bathrooms, utility rooms, doors, windows, and trim, high-gloss paints are ideal. Semigloss paints, with less resin and a reduced surface shine, are slightly less wear-resistant but still suitable for most woodwork. Finally, flat paints are the coating of choice for most interior walls and ceilings because they provide an attractive, low-glare finish for surfaces that take little abuse and require only infrequent washings. Here's a paint primer to help you decide what kind of paint you need for the quick fix at hand.

Latex Paint

The word "latex" originally referred to the use of rubber in one form or another as the resin, or solid, in paint. The solvent or thinner, called the "vehicle," was water. Today, many paints are made with water as the thinner but with resins that are not latex, and the industry is leaning toward such terms as "water-thinned" or "water-reducible." If the paints are called latex at all, the term often used is "acrylic latex" because they contain a plastic resin made of acrylics or polyvinyls rather than rubber.

In addition to the speed of drying, new opacity, and washability of acrylic latex paints, the greatest advantage of water-thinned paints is you can clean up with water. The higher expense—as well as the potential fire hazard—of volatile thinners and brush cleaners is gone. If you wash the brush or roller immediately after the painting session is over, it comes clean in just a few minutes.

Latex paint works well on surfaces previously painted with latex or flat oilbase paints. It can even be used on unprimed drywall or unpainted masonry. However, latex usually does not adhere well to high-gloss finishes, and, even though it can be used on wallpaper, there is a risk that the water in the paint may cause the paper to peel away from the wall. Because of its water content, latex will cause bare steel to rust and will raise the grain on raw wood.

Alkyd Resin Paint

The use of synthetic alkyd resin for solvent-thinned (oil-base) paints has brought several advantages. One of the most useful is a special formula that makes the paint yogurt-thick. A brush dipped in it carries more paint to the surface than previous versions. Yet, under the friction of application, the paint spreads and smooths readily.

INTERIOR PAINTS

Type	Characteristics/Use	Application
Acoustic	For acoustic ceiling tile. Water-thinned, water cleanup.	Spray (preferable) or roller.
Alkyd	Solvent-thinned, solvent cleanup. Don't apply over unprimed drywall.	Brush, roller, pad.
Cement	For concrete, brick, stucco. Some contain waterproofing agents. Must be mixed just before use.	Brush.
Dripless	For ceilings. More costly than ordinary paints.	Brush or roller.
Epoxy	For metal, glass, tile, floors, woodwork: high-stress areas. Expensive. May require special mixing; tricky to use.	Brush.
Latex	Most popular. Water-thinned, water cleanup. Gloss, semigloss, flat. May be used over most surfaces but not on wallpaper, wood, or metal.	Brush, roller, pad.
Metal	For bare or primed metal or as a primer for other types of paint. Some water-thinned, most solvent-thinned.	Brush or spray.
Oil	Slow-drying, strong odor. Coverage may not be as good as synthetic paints. Solvent-thinned, solvent cleanup.	Brush, roller, spray.
One-coat	Water- or solvent-thinned. Costs more than regular latex or alkyd. Surface must be sealed first. Excellent covering power.	Brush, roller, pad.
Polyurethane/Urethane	Expensive. Can be used over most finishes, porous surfaces. Extreme durability. Solvents, primers vary.	Brush.
Textured	Good for covering surface defects. Premixed or mix-at-home types. Application slow. Permits surface design of choice.	Brush, roller, pad, trowel, sponge.

In most gloss and semigloss (or satin) paints, alkyd materials are still preferred for trim, doors, and even heavy-traffic hallways. Many homeowners still like them best for bathrooms and kitchens.

The opacity of alkyd paints has improved with the addition of a material that diffuses and evaporates, which leaves minute bubbles that reflect and scatter light and makes the paint look thicker than it really is. With paints of this formula, one coat of white will completely cover black or bright yellow.

While alkyds should not be used on unprimed drywall (they can raise the nap of its paper coating) or on unprimed masonry, they are suitable for raw wood and for almost any previously painted or wallpapered surface. The most durable of interior paints, alkyds are dry enough for a second coat within four to six hours. Solvents must be used for thinning and cleanup. Check the label to find which solvent is recommended by the paint manufacturer. And, while the solvents may be almost odorless, they're still toxic and flammable, so you should work in a well-ventilated room.

Textured Paint

If you're after a finish that looks like stucco, or if you want an effective cover-up for flawed surfaces, textured-surface paint will do the job. Some varieties come premixed with sandlike particles suspended in the paint. Because of their grittiness, these paints are usually used on ceilings, where they will not rub off. With other varieties, you have to add the particles and stir thoroughly. Another form of textured paint has no granules. Thick and smooth, it's applied to the surface and then textured with special tools. Textured paints are available in either flat-finish latex or alkyd formulations. Latex versions are frequently used on bare drywall ceilings because they can be used without a primer and they help to camouflage the seams between sheets of drywall.

One of the problems with textured paint becomes evident when the time comes to paint over it. All those peaks and valleys created by the texturing actually increase the surface area of the wall. The rough surface will require 15 to 25 percent more paint the second time around.

Dripless Paint

More expensive than conventional alkyd paint, dripless paint is ideal for ceilings because it's so thick it won't run off a roller or brush. It will usually cover any surface in a single coat, but, because it's so dense, it won't go as far as its more spreadable relatives.

One-Coat Paint

With additional pigment to improve their covering capabilities, true one-coats are otherwise just more expensive versions of ordinary latex or alkyd paints. For best results, reserve them for use on flawless, same-color surfaces that have been previously sealed. **Tip:** Not all paints advertised as "one-coat" really are. Read the warranty.

Primers

Primers are inexpensive undercoatings that smooth out uneven surfaces, provide a barrier between porous surfaces and certain finishing coats, and allow you to use an otherwise incompatible paint on a bare or previously painted surface. For flat paint finishes, the primer can be a thinned-out version of the paint itself. But that's often more expensive than using a premixed primer, which contains less-expensive pigment, dries quickly, and provides a firm foundation, or "tooth," for the final coat of paint. Latex primer has all the advantages of latex paint—almost odor-free, quick-drying, and easy to clean up—and is the best undercoat for drywall, plaster, and concrete. Don't use it on bare wood, though, because the water in it may raise the grain. For raw wood, it's best to use an alkyd primer.

ABRASIVES

Choosing the proper abrasive for a given job usually means the difference between mediocre results and a professional-looking appearance. Depending on the job, you'll choose among sandpaper, steel wool, or a file.

Sandpaper

There are four factors to consider when selecting any coated abrasive: the abrasive mineral, or which type of rough material; the grade, or the coarseness or fineness of the mineral; the backing (paper or cloth); and the coating, or the nature and extent of the mineral on the surface.

Paper backing for coated abrasives comes in four weights: A, C, D, and E. A (also referred to as "Finishing") is the lightest weight and is designed for light sanding work. C and D (also called "Cabinet") are for heavier work, while E is for the toughest jobs. The coating can be either open or closed. Open coated means the grains are spaced to only cover a portion of the surface. An open-coated abrasive is best used on gummy or soft woods, on soft metals, or on painted surfaces. Closed coated means the abrasive covers the entire area. They provide maximum cutting, but they also clog faster and are best used on hard woods and metals.

There are three popular ways to grade coated abrasives. Simplified markings (coarse, medium, fine, very fine, etc.) provide a general description of the grade. The grit refers to the number of mineral grains that, when set end to end, equal 1 inch. The commonly used O symbols are more or less arbitrary. The coarsest grading under this system is $4\frac{1}{2}$, and the finest is $^{10}\!/\!0$, or 0000000000.

Steel Wool

Steel wool comes in many grades of coarseness. Always apply the correct grade of steel wool to the work you have at hand.

Files

A wood rasp, with a rasp and/or curved-tooth cut, is used to remove excess wood. The piece of wood is final-smoothed with a single-cut or double-cut file. You may not need files for most quick fixes. If you decide to add some to your quick fix toolbox, buy an assortment of flat files—wood rasp, bastard, second-cut, and smooth.

QUICK FIX SAFETY

Performing quick fixes around your home should be satisfying and safe. (You won't feel satisfied if you have to visit the emergency room because of a cut or fall!) Choose safe tools, learn how to use them correctly, and employ safety equipment to avoid injuries.

SAFE TOOLS

The first rule of tool safety is to buy good quality, as suggested at the beginning of this book. You don't have to buy the best, but lowest cost often means lowest value.

SAFE LADDERS

Most home-use ladders are made of wood or aluminum. Depending on quality, both types are reliable. Aluminum, however, weighs only 20 to 50 percent as much as wood, which means it's easier to take it in and out of storage or move it around. On most good ladders you'll find labels that indicate a rated strength. For example, a Type I industrial-grade ladder, rated at 250 pounds, is the strongest. A Type II commercial-grade ladder is rated at 225 pounds; Type III is rated at 200 pounds. Fortunately, each type has actually been successfully tested at four times its rated load. For around-the-house purposes, invest in security and durability and buy a Type II ladder. One that's 6 feet tall will do for most homeowners, but taller ones are available. For an extra measure of safety, get one with rubber or plastic feet so your ladder won't skid on hard floors.

If you're painting a ceiling from a single stepladder, you'll find yourself going up and down like a yo-yo, constantly moving the ladder to reach unpainted areas. A safer alternative is to buy a second ladder of the same size. Then, using

QUICK FIX TOOL CARE

Quality tools aren't cheap. Fortunately, with care, they can last many years and be a better long-term investment than cheap tools. Here are some useful tips on tool care.

- Protect your tools from moisture. Keep a thin coating of oil on metal parts, wrap them in plastic wrap, or keep carpenters' chalk or mothballs (both of which absorb moisture) in your toolbox.
- A piece of garden hose slit open is a handy protective cover for the teeth of a handsaw between projects. Circular saw blades store conveniently in heavy shipping envelopes.
- To remind yourself to unplug an electric drill when changing accessories, fasten the chuck key near the plug end of the cord.
- Tack rags will last longer if they're stored in an airtight container to keep them from drying out. Airtight storage also prevents spontaneous combustion, which can be very dangerous. (This safety tip applies equally well to other rags, coveralls, work gloves, and any other clothes that might absorb flammable oils and solvents.)
- Don't take a chance of hitting a thumb or finger when hammering a small brad, tack, or nail. Slip the fastener between the teeth of a pocket comb; the comb holds the nail while you hold the comb. A bobby pin or a paper clip can be used in the same way.

a pair of 2×8-foot boards, make a scaffold between them—a platform from which you can paint for longer periods of time by moving from one end of the bridge to the other. Don't make your scaffold higher than is absolutely necessary and no longer than 6 to 8 feet in length. Use C-clamps to fasten each end of the 2×8s to a rung of each ladder.

Using Ladders Safely

There's no such thing as an absolutely safe ladder. Gravity is always an unrelenting enemy. However, there are ways to greatly reduce your risk of accidents and injury.

- Always open a stepladder to its fullest position, lock the spreader braces on each side in place, and pull down the bucket shelf.

- Always face the ladder head-on, and use both hands to hold onto the side rails or rungs.

- Don't climb higher than two rungs from the top of the ladder; don't sit or stand on the top or the bucket shelf.

- To keep yourself from overreaching and getting off balance, never let your navel go beyond the ladder's side rails.

- If you must work on a ladder in front of a door, lock it first.

- Put the paint can or tray on the bucket shelf before you climb the ladder. And don't go up the ladder with tools in your hand or in your pockets.

OTHER SAFETY TIPS

Need some more safety tips? Sure you do. Fortunately, most of them are built on good old common sense.

- Quick doesn't mean "work as fast as you can move." It means planning out the task in advance and doing it safely and well.

- Don't change a power-saw blade or bit without first unplugging the cord or disconnecting the battery pack.

- Wear latex gloves when working with adhesives so you don't bond your fingers together.

- Before you replace or repair any electrical fixture, deenergize the electrical circuit by turning off the appropriate circuit breaker or removing the circuit fuse.

- Wear a painter's mask, particularly if you are using alkyd paints indoors. When painting overhead, wear goggles.

- Wear safety glasses when sanding, filing, or doing any job that produces flying particles.

QUICK WALL FIXES

Walls and ceilings make up about 80 percent of a home's interior surfaces, so knowing how to make repairs to them can be very helpful to a homeowner. Best of all, you can make many of these repairs more quickly and easily than you might think. Here are some quick fixes you can tackle on your own, including how to remove and install the molding that adds a finished touch to your walls, windows, and doors.

FIXING POPPED NAILS

In most newer homes, the walls are surfaced with gypsum wallboard, also known as drywall (see page 20 for an overview of this popular building material). Drywall, like all building materials, has its own characteristics and problems. One of the most common problems results from shrinking or warping in the framing behind the drywall. As the wood studs age and shrink, nails loosen and pop out of the wood, producing an unsightly bump or hole in the surface. No matter how many times you drive the nails back into the drywall, the problem is likely to recur, so it's better to fix it permanently the first time around. Here's how to fix popped nails:

1. Redrive popped nails. If nails are sticking out far enough to get claw of hammer around them, pull them out first. To redrive them, hold nail set over nail head and hammer nail as far as you can into stud. Nail head will punch through drywall's outside layer of paper and into drywall itself.

2. To be sure nail stays in place (and to take pressure off it), drive another drywall nail through wallboard and into stud about 2 inches above

What You'll Need

Hammer
Nail set
Drywall nails
Putty knife
Spackling compound
Sandpaper
Paint or primer
Paintbrushes

or below old nail. Pound nail flush with wall and then give it one more light hammer whack to "dimple" drywall surface around nail head.

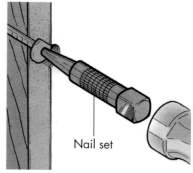

Nail set

3. Using putty knife, cover new nail head and fill hole over old one with spackling compound.

Nail pops in drywall are easy to eliminate. First drive the popped nail with a nail set as far as possible into the stud. Then drive another nail about 2 inches above or below it.

4. Let dry, then lightly sand area. Since spackling compound shrinks as it dries, you may need to repeat process once or twice more. Touch up patches with paint or primer.

FIXING HOLES IN DRYWALL

Tough as it is, drywall can withstand only limited abuse. Flinging a door open with too much force can produce a doorknob-size hole in the wall. This kind of damage looks bad, but even large holes are easy to fix. The easiest way is to purchase a drywall repair kit. Measure the hole, and visit your local hardware store or home improvement center for a kit. There are various sizes and types for different applications. For example, a drywall patch for a ceiling is thicker than one for a wall. Before you use the kit, remove any loose paper or plaster around the edges of the hole. Then apply drywall patch, following the manufacturer's instructions.

Small Drywall Hole

To make a repair to a small drywall hole without a kit:

1. Prepare tin can lid that is at least 1½ inches greater in diameter than hole in drywall for backing piece. Use

keyhole saw to cut out narrow horizontal slit in wall on each side of hole. Measurement of hole plus both narrow slits should equal diameter of lid so you can insert lid sideways into hole.

2. Use awl to punch two holes in center of lid. Thread 12-inch piece of wire or string through holes.

3. Holding ends of wire, slide lid through slit. Still holding wire, pull lid toward you until it's flat against inside of wall. To hold in place, set stick of scrap wood over hole on outside of wall and twist wire tightly over stick. Can lid should be held firmly against inside of wall.

4. Use putty knife to apply premixed drywall patching compound over patch following manufacturer's instructions. (Don't use spackling compound because it shrinks as it dries.) You can also mix plaster of paris with water to make thick paste. Pack compound or plaster into hole against backing and behind stick. Keep compound inside hole, cover backing, and fill slits, but don't spread it on wall surface. Leave patch slightly low, and don't try to level it. Let patch dry until it turns bright white, typically at least 24 hours. When dry, cut string or wire and remove stick.

5. To finish patch, fill it completely with more plaster of paris or drywall patching compound to make patch level with wall surface. Let dry, lightly sand area, prime, and paint.

Large Drywall Hole

Sometimes a wall can get a large hole or a section can be damaged by water or other causes. Here's how to fix it without a drywall repair kit:

What You'll Need

Clean tin can lid
Tape measure
Keyhole saw
Awl
Thin wire or string
Scissors or wire cutters
Scrap wood
Putty knife
Drywall patching
  compound
Sandpaper
Primer and paint
Paintbrushes

What You'll Need

Scrap piece of drywall
Utility knife
Pencil
Keyhole saw
Small board
Flathead screws
Screwdriver
Spackling or wallboard
    joint compound
Putty knife
Sandpaper
Primer and paint
Paintbrushes

1. Cut scrap piece of drywall with utility knife into square or rectangle. Scrap piece should be a little bigger than hole or damaged area. If you don't have piece of drywall, purchase drywall patch from hardware store. Set patch against damaged area, and lightly trace around it with pencil. Cut out outlined area with keyhole saw. Keep saw cut on inside of traced line so hole in drywall will be exactly the same size as patch.

2. To hold wallboard patch in place, install small board about 6 inches longer than long dimension of hole. Put board into hole, center it horizontally, and hold it firmly against inside of wallboard. To help keep it there, fasten ends of board to drywall with flathead screws driven through wall at sides of hole; countersink screws below surface of drywall.

3. Use spackling compound or wallboard joint compound as glue to hold patch in place. Spread compound on back of drywall patch and around edges. Set patch into hole and adjust it so it's exactly even with surrounding wall. Hold it in place until compound starts to set. Let compound dry at least overnight.

4. Once compound is dry, fill patch outline and cover exposed screw heads with spackling or joint compound. Let dry, lightly sand area, prime, and paint.

Secure a backing board on the inside of the wall to brace the patch; then coat the edges of the patch with spackling compound and set it into place in the hole.

FIXING CERAMIC WALL TILE

Tiles crack or loosen, and the grout between them wears down and crumbles. If you don't fix the damage, water can seep behind the tiles and cause more serious trouble. To keep the problem from getting worse, make the repairs as soon as you can.

Replacing Tile

If you can't find a tile that matches, try salvage yards for an old one. To replace a tile:

What You'll Need

Masking tape
Safety goggles
Electric drill with carbide bit
Glass cutter
Chisel
Hammer
Scraper
Replacement tile
Ceramic mastic
Putty knife or notched
   spreader
Tape or toothpicks
Rubber gloves
Ceramic tile grout
Clean sponges or towels

1. Remove old tile by putting piece of masking tape at its center. Then, wearing safety goggles, drill hole into taped spot with carbide bit. Peel off tape, and score an *X* across tile with glass cutter. Break up tile with chisel and hammer; remove pieces.

2. Use scraper or chisel to remove old adhesive and grout from wall. Be sure there's no loose grout around opening.

3. Spread ceramic mastic on back of new tile with putty knife or notched spreader, leaving tile edges clean.

4. Carefully set new tile into opening on wall. Press tile in firmly, moving it slightly from side to side to distribute mastic, until it's flush with surrounding surface. Space around tile should be even, and tile should be perfectly aligned. Use tape or toothpicks around edge of tile to hold it in place. Let mastic cure according to manufacturer's instructions.

5. Remove tape holding tile in place. Wear rubber gloves as you mix ceramic tile grout to fill joints around tile,

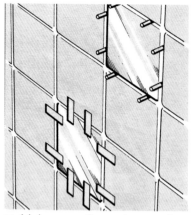

Hold the new tile in place with tape or toothpicks.

following manufacturer's instructions. Use damp sponge to apply grout all around new tile, filling gaps completely.

6. Let set for 15 minutes, then wipe wall with clean, damp sponge or towel. Be careful not to disturb grout around new tile. Let grout dry completely—at least 12 hours.

7. Once grout is dry, firmly rub tile with damp towel to remove any remaining grout from wall.

Regrouting Tile

Crumbling grout should be replaced as soon as possible to prevent mildew and water damage. To regrout tile:

What You'll Need

Household cleaner
Clean sponges and towels
Chlorine bleach
Old toothbrush
Putty knife
Vacuum cleaner
Rubber gloves
Ceramic tile grout
Silicone tile grout spray

1. Scrub tile thoroughly with strong household cleaner. Rinse well. If old grout is mildewed, remove mildew before you regrout by scrubbing tile joints with old toothbrush dipped in chlorine bleach. Rinse thoroughly.

2. Remove all crumbling grout you can with edge of putty knife, then vacuum. Rinse wall to be sure it's absolutely clean, but don't dry it. Wall should be damp when new grout is applied.

3. Wearing rubber gloves, mix ceramic tile grout according to manufacturer's instructions. Apply grout with damp sponge, firmly wiping it in areas that need grouting to fill joints. Smooth newly grouted joints with clean, damp sponge. As necessary, add more grout, and smooth it again, filling tile joints completely.

4. Let dry for at least 12 hours. Then scrub wall firmly with clean dry towel to remove any grout that's left on tiles. Seal tile joints with silicone tile grout spray.

REPLACING MOLDING

Moldings are wood trim around doors, windows, and wall perimeters, such as between a wall and floor or wall and ceiling. Moldings not only make your rooms look finished, but they also protect your walls and doorways, absorbing bumps and scrapes before they get to the walls, kind of like car bumpers. Because baseboards are at floor level where they can be struck by all sorts of objects, they are the most easily damaged moldings. Read on to learn how to replace baseboard molding; you can apply the same techniques to other types of moldings as well.

Removing Molding

Before you install fresh molding, you must remove the old molding. Here's how:

What You'll Need

Putty knife
Short pry bar
Wood block
Small cedar shingle
  wedges
Hammer

1. Remove any shoe molding (quarter-round piece of wood that fits against both baseboard and floor). Because it's nailed to subfloor, gently pry with putty knife at one end of shoe molding to get it started. Then, use short pry bar and wood block for leverage. Once started, shoe molding should come up easily.

2. Pry off damaged baseboard. To do this, start at one end and insert small, flat pry bar between baseboard and wall. Pry gently, and move farther down molding whenever you can, slipping small cedar shingle wedges into any

gaps. Work all the way along baseboard, prying and wedging. Then work back between wedges, tapping wedges in deeper as baseboard comes out. Continue until molding comes off.

3. Check to see if any nails have been pulled through either shoe molding or baseboard. If so, pull out nails completely.

To remove a baseboard, pry it with a pry bar, then use a wedge.

Using Miter Box

If the old baseboard came off intact, you can use it as a pattern for cutting the new one. If part of it is missing or badly damaged, however, you will have to use a miter box to cut the new moldings without the aid of a pattern. An inexpensive wooden or plastic miter box is adequate for this work. Slots in the box allow you to cut molding at 45° angles. Use either a backsaw or a fine-tooth blade in a hacksaw to do the sawing. Before sawing, place the molding you are about to cut next to the molding it will rest against to be sure the cut is the correct one. The following steps instruct you on how to make two 45° cuts and to join two pieces of molding so they form a right angle:

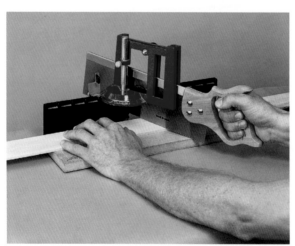

Use a miter box and a backsaw to make 45° cuts.

1. Place length of molding in miter box, mak-

ing sure lip of miter box presses against edge of table or bench so you can keep it steady.

2. Hold molding tightly against side of miter box to prevent it from slipping as you saw 45° cut at one end.

3. Repeat procedure for other length of molding. Two lengths should form a perfect right angle.

What You'll Need

Replacement molding
Miter box
Backsaw or hacksaw

Installing Molding

When you finish cutting all the mitered joints, you are ready to install the new baseboard molding and reinstall the shoe molding.

1. Cut molding to size, then paint or stain it. To be sure you don't damage finish, you may want to paint or stain moldings after you've installed them on your walls.

2. Fit all pieces together before nailing to ensure you cut molding correctly.

3. Locate wall studs. If you're replacing molding, they should be where old molding was nailed.

4. Nail baseboard in place with finishing nails, then use nail set to drive nail heads below surface of molding.

5. Install shoe molding with finishing nails. Shoe molding, however, must be nailed to floor and not to baseboard.

What You'll Need

Finish molding
Miter box
Backsaw
Paint or stain
Paintbrushes
Stud finder
Finishing nails
Hammer
Nail set

Drive nail heads below surface of shoe molding with nail set.

QUICK FLOOR FIXES

When you consider the punishment caused by everyday foot traffic, it's surprising that floors hold up as well as they do. Eventually wear and tear take their toll. Fortunately, there are quick fixes for most floor problems.

FIXING SQUEAKY FLOORS

If your floors are exposed hardwood, you may be able to stop the squeak by sprinkling talcum powder over the noisy boards and sweeping it back and forth to force it down into the cracks. The powder will lubricate the edges of the boards, eliminating the noise. Following are some more permanent ways to solve squeaky problems.

From under the floor, drive wedges into gaps between the subflooring and the joists to stop squeaks.

If there's a basement or crawl space under the noisy floor, work from this area to locate the problem. You'll need a helper upstairs to walk on the squeaky spot while you work. Watch the subfloor under the noisy boards while your helper steps on the floor above. If the subfloor moves visibly or if you can pinpoint the noise, outline the affected areas with chalk. At the joists closest to your outlines, look for gaps between the joist and the subfloor; wherever there's a gap, the floorboards can move. To stop squeaks here, install shingles or wood shims into the gaps to reduce movement.

If there are no gaps along the joists, or if the squeaks are coming from an area between joists, there's probably a gap between the floorboards and the subfloor. To pull the two layers together, install wood screws up through the subflooring in the squeaky areas. Make sure you drill pilot holes before inserting the screws so you don't crack the wood. The wood screws must be long enough to penetrate into the floor above you but not so long that they go all the way through the boards and stick up through your floor.

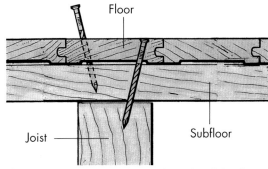

If you cannot access the underside of the floor, angle flooring nails from above into a joist, then fill nail holes with wood putty.

If you can't get at the floor from underneath, you'll have to work from the top with spiral flooring nails. First, locate the squeak and try to determine whether it's at a joist or between joists. To eliminate the squeak, drive two spiral flooring nails, angled toward each other in a V, through the floorboards and the subfloor. If the squeak is at a joist, use longer spiral flooring nails, driving them through the floorboards and the subfloor and into the joist. Drill pilot holes first to keep the boards from splitting.

If the floor is tiled or carpeted and you can't get at the floorboards from above or below, try to reset the loose boards by pounding. Using a hammer and a block of scrap wood as a buffer, pound the floor firmly in an area about 2 or 3 feet square over the squeaky boards. The pressure of the pounding may force loose nails back into place.

FIXING TILE FLOORS

If a tile is loose, it can be reglued with floor tile adhesive. If it's just loose at one edge or corner, cover the tile with aluminum foil and then with a clean cloth. Heat the loose edges with an iron set to medium heat to soften the old adhesive and rebond it. When the adhesive has softened, put weights over the entire tile and let the adhesive cure for several hours or overnight.

If the old adhesive isn't strong enough to reattach the tile, use a floor tile adhesive made for that type of tile. Heat the tile as described above, and carefully lift the loose edges with a paint scraper or a putty knife. Scrape the old adhesive off the edges, and apply a thin coat of new adhesive, using a notched spreader or trowel. Smooth the tile firmly from center to edges, and put weight on the entire tile. Let the adhesive cure as directed by the manufacturer.

To replace a damaged tile, heat the tile as described above, and carefully pry it up with a paint scraper or a putty knife. Scrape all the old adhesive off the floor, and fill any gouges in the tile base with wood filler. Let the filler dry completely.

Check the fit of the new tile in the prepared opening. If the new tile doesn't fit exactly, sand the edges or carefully slice off the excess with a sharp utility knife and a straightedge. When the tile fits perfectly, spread a thin coat of floor tile adhesive in the opening, using a notched trowel or spreader. Warm the new tile with an iron to make it flexible, then carefully set it into place in the opening, pressing it firmly onto the adhesive. Weight the entire tile, and let the adhesive cure as directed by the manufacturer.

FIXING SHEET FLOORS

When a floor is badly worn or damaged, use scrap flooring to patch it. You'll need a piece of flooring a little bigger than the bad spot, with the same pattern.

1. Position flooring scrap over bad spot so it covers damaged area completely and so pattern is aligned exactly with floor pattern.

2. Affix scrap firmly in place on floor, using package sealing tape all around edges. Then, with straight-edge and sharp utility knife, cut rectangle through scrap piece and through flooring below it to make patch bigger than damaged area. Cut along joints or lines in pattern, if possible, to make patch harder to see. Be sure corners are cleanly cut.

3. Once flooring is cut through, untape scrap piece and push out rectangular patch. Soften old flooring inside cut lines by heating it with iron, set to medium heat. Cover patch area with aluminum foil and then with clean cloth; press until adhesive underneath has softened. Carefully pry up damaged piece with paint scraper or putty knife. Scrape all old adhesive off floor to make clean base for patch. If there are any gouges in floor, fill them with water putty. Let dry completely.

4. Install patch in opening. If it binds a little, you can sand edges slightly to adjust the fit. When patch fits exactly, spread thin coat of floor tile adhesive in opening with notched trowel or spreader. Then set patch into gap, press in firmly, and wipe off any excess adhesive around edges.

5. Heat-seal edges to main sheet of flooring. Protect floor with aluminum foil and clean cloth, as above; press edges firmly but quickly with hot iron.

6. After bonding edges, place weight over entire patch and let adhesive cure as directed by manufacturer. Don't wash floor for at least a week.

What You'll Need

Matching flooring
 for patching
Package sealing tape
Utility knife
Straightedge
Iron
Aluminum foil
Clean cloth
Paint scraper or
 putty knife
Water putty
Medium- or fine-grade
 sandpaper
Floor tile adhesive
Notched trowel or
 spreader
Weights

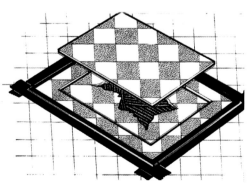

Use a piece of scrap flooring as a patch for damaged flooring.

QUICK DOOR FIXES

Doors are great—when they work. But what if a door is sticking or won't entirely close? Or perhaps you want to replace a door with a different style or type. Fixing or replacing a door is relatively easy and usually requires only a few common tools and a couple hours of your time.

UNSTICKING DOORS

Doors, like windows, stick for a number of reasons—from poor construction to extreme humidity. In most cases, it's easy to unstick a stubborn door. To diagnose the problem, close the door, watching it carefully to locate the binding point. If there's a gap between the door and the frame opposite the binding edge, the hinges probably need adjustment. If you can't see a gap anywhere between the door and the frame and you had to slam the door to close it, the wood has probably swollen from extreme humidity. If the hinges and the wood are both in good shape, the door frame itself may be out of alignment; check the frame with a carpenters' square.

To fix a door with poorly adjusted hinges, examine the hinges for loose screws, both on the door and on the frame. Securely tighten any loose screws. If a screw doesn't tighten, the screw hole has become enlarged. When the hole is only slightly enlarged, you may be able to correct the problem by replacing the screw with a longer one, but make sure the head is the same size.

Another option is to use a hollow fiber plug with the old screw. To do this, spread carpenters' glue on the outside of the plug, and insert the fiber plug into the enlarged screw hole. Then drive the screw into the hole. If the screw hole is badly enlarged, you can use wood toothpicks to fill it in. Loose hinge screws can also be tightened by filling the hole with wooden toothpicks dipped in glue and trimmed flush. Dip the toothpicks into carpenters' glue and insert them around the screw hole. Let the glue dry, then trim the toothpicks flush with the surface. When you drive the screw into the filled-in hole, it should hold securely.

If the screws are not loose, the hinges on the door frame may have to be readjusted. Close the door, watching to see where it sticks and where it gaps. If the door is tilted in the frame, it will stick at the top on one side and at the bottom on the other, and there will be a gap between the door and the frame opposite each binding point.

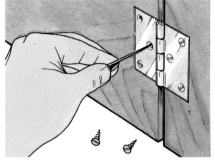

Loose hinge screws can be tightened by filling the hole with wooden toothpicks dipped in glue and trimmed flush.

If the door hinges need shimming, open the door as far as it will go. Push a wedge under it to hold it firmly. At the hinge to be adjusted, loosen the screws from the hinge leaf on the door frame, but don't touch the screws in the door itself. Cut a piece of thin cardboard to the same size as the hinge leaf, and mark the location of the hinge screws on it. Cut horizontal slots in the shim to fit over the screws; slide the shim over the screws behind the loosened hinge leaf. Keeping the shim in place, tighten the screws to resecure the hinge. Remove the wedge holding the door and close the door. If the door still sticks, but not as much as it did before, add another shim under the hinge.

If the door sticks even after shimming, or if there is no gap anywhere around the frame, you'll have to remove some wood at the binding points. Use a block plane on the top or bottom of the door or a jack plane to work on the side.

If the door sticks at the sides, try to plane only on the hinge side; the latch side is beveled slightly, and planing could damage the bevel. Use the plane carefully, removing only a little wood at a time. Keep your cuts even across the entire binding edge.

If the door sticks because the frame is out of alignment, there's not much you can do to fix it. At the binding point, set a piece of 2×4 flat against the frame, and give it several firm hammer blows. This may move the frame just enough to solve the problem. If this doesn't work, you'll have to adjust the hinges or plane the edges to allow for the unevenness of the frame. The door may end up slightly crooked, but it won't stick.

REPLACING INTERIOR DOORS

Hanging or installing a door isn't as difficult as it may seem. In fact, you probably can tackle this quick fix in an hour or two if you have the necessary materials and tools ready.

Installing Prehung Doors

Prehung doors are the easiest to install. To buy a prehung door, you need to know the size of the rough door opening. There are approximately 3 inches at the side jambs and 1½ inches at the head jamb for fitting purposes. To install a prehung door:

What You'll Need

Prehung door
Level
Cedar shingle shims
Hammer
16d finishing nails
Nail set
Wood putty
10d finishing nails
Wood sealer

1. Set door into rough opening and vertically level, or plumb, door jamb sides, filling any gaps at top and sides with cedar shingle shims.

2. Nail head and side jambs to rough framing, using 16d finishing nails. Countersink heads into face of jambs with nail set. Fill holes with putty.

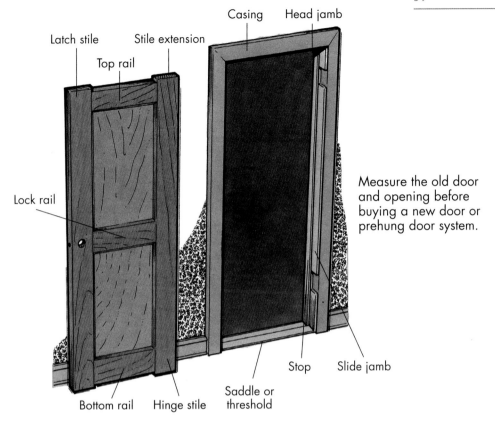

Casing   Head jamb

Latch stile   Stile extension

Top rail

Lock rail

Measure the old door and opening before buying a new door or prehung door system.

Stop   Slide jamb

Saddle or threshold

Bottom rail   Hinge stile

3. Nail finished casing or molding to doorway with 10d finishing nails. Countersink nail heads, and fill with wood putty.

4. Apply wood sealer to both sides of door and top, bottom, and side edges. Seal casing and door moldings too.

Installing Locksets

Once you've hung a new door, you need to fit it with a lockset. Some doors come predrilled for standard-size locksets. Other doors require you to drill the holes yourself, using a template provided by the lock manufacturer. With some doors, you need to cut mortises, or holes, in the door edge for the lockset and in the frame for the strike plate that engages the lock's bolt. Here's how:

What You'll Need

Lockset
Tape
Pencil
Power drill with
    hole-saw attachment
Combination square
Sandpaper
Chisel
Screwdriver

1. Wrap paper or cardboard template that comes with new lockset around edge of door according to manufacturer's instructions. Template will be used to locate two holes: one hole for lock cylinder and the other for edge of door for bolt. Mark centers for these two holes on door.

2. Use power drill with hole-saw attachment to drill hole the size specified for lock cylinder. When you see point of drill coming through, stop and finish boring from other side.

3. Drill hole the appropriate size for bolt into edge of door until you reach cylinder hole. Use combination square against edge of door and drill bit to keep bit at right angle to door. Smooth edges of holes with sandpaper.

4. Insert bolt into hole, and place bolt plate in position over it. Trace bolt plate's outline on edge of door. Follow manufacturer's instructions to remove bolt and mortise edge for bolt plate so it will be flush with surface.

5. Use chisel to cut mortise. Insert bolt and plate in mortise, and drill pilot holes for mounting screws. Install screws to secure bolt in place.

6. Insert outside lock cylinder so connecting bar fits into bolt assembly. Attach interior lock cylinder, and secure it with screws.

7. Locate proper spot for strike plate on jamb, and drill proper-size hole in

Install the outside lock cylinder so the connecting bar fits into the bolt assembly.

jamb. Using strike plate as pattern, mark jamb for mortis-ing, and cut mortise. Install strike plate with screws so it fits flush with jamb.

OTHER QUICK DOOR FIX TIPS

- If you're trying to remove a door's hinge pin and the pin won't budge, press a nail against the hinge bottom and tap upward against the nail with a hammer.

- For better control when lifting a door off its hinges, remove the bottom pin first. When replacing a door on its hinges, insert the top pin first.

- You won't need to worry about oil dripping on the floor if you quiet a squeaky hinge by lubricating its pin with petroleum jelly rather than oil.

- If you need to plane the bottom of a door because it scrapes the threshold or the floor, you can do so without removing the door. Place sandpaper on the threshold or floor, then move the door back and forth over this abrasive surface. Slide a newspaper or magazine under the sand-paper if it needs to be raised in order to make contact.

- To remove ¼ inch or more from a door, score with a utility knife to prevent chipping, and finish with a circular saw.

- When you've fashioned a door to the exact size for hang-ing, bevel the latch edge backward to let it clear the jamb as it swings open and shut.

- Before you replace a door that you have planed, seal the planed edges with wood sealer. If you don't, the door will swell and stick again.

QUICK WINDOW FIXES

Windows are often trouble spots. Along with doors, windows are the major source of heat-loss in most homes. They also may stick shut when they're painted or swell shut from humidity. Inside, shades and venetian blinds may not work right, glass gets broken, and screens get torn. Fortunately, there's a lot you can do to keep your windows working properly.

UNSTICKING WINDOWS

Double-hung wood-frame windows, especially in older homes, often stick. The most common cause of this problem is that the window has been painted shut and the paint has sealed it closed. The solution is usually simple: Break the seal, and clear and lubricate the sash tracks. Unsticking a window takes strength, but it isn't difficult. Here's how:

1. Before you start to work, make sure window is unlocked.

What You'll Need

Stiff putty knife
　　or paint scraper
Hammer
Chisel
Medium-grade sandpaper
Sanding block
Silicone lubricant
Block of scrap wood
Small pry bar

2. Look for evidence of a paint seal between sash and window frame. To break seal, push blade of stiff putty knife or paint scraper into joint, cutting straight in through paint. If necessary, lightly tap knife with hammer to force blade in. If window was painted on outside, repeat procedure to break seal on outside.

3. If window still doesn't open, check tracks in window frame above sash; they're probably blocked with built-up paint. Using hammer and chisel, carefully clean excess paint out of tracks. Cut out thickened paint, but be careful not to gouge the wood of the tracks. Smooth cleaned-out tracks with sandpaper on a narrow sanding block, then spray them with silicone lubricant.

4. If window still sticks, the paint in lower part of tracks is probably holding it. Set block of scrap wood against sash at window frame. Gently tap block of wood with hammer to force sash back from frame. Move block of wood all around window sash, tapping sash back from frame; then try window again. If it opens, clean and sand tracks, and lubricate them with silicone spray.

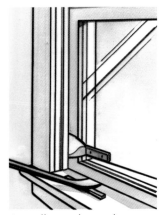

A really stuck window may require using a small pry bar to open it.

5. If window still doesn't open, use small pry bar on it, preferably from outside. Insert flat end of pry bar under sash; set block of scrap wood under it for better leverage. Pry gently at corners of sash and then from corners in toward center. Use pry bar very carefully; too much pressure could damage both sash and frame. If window opens, clean and lubricate tracks with silicone spray. If it still doesn't open, sticking may be caused by extreme humidity, poor construction, or uneven settling. Call carpenter to fix window rather than trying to force it open.

REPLACING BROKEN OR CRACKED GLASS

Broken glass is one of the easiest problems to fix. You can buy replacement glass, cut to measure, at lumberyards and larger hardware stores. Here's how to replace a broken pane in a single pane (one thickness of glass) window:

1. Wearing safety goggles and gloves, remove broken or cracked glass from window frame. To remove glass without excessive splintering, crisscross pane on both sides with masking tape, then rap it with a hammer. Most

What You'll Need

Safety goggles
Heavy gloves
Masking tape
Hammer
Chisel or scraper
Linseed oil
Clean cloth
Tape measure
Replacement glass
Glaziers' points or spring clips
Putty knife
Glaziers' compound or putty
Single-edge razor blade
    or glass scraper
Rust-resistant paint
    and paintbrush

of the pane will be held together. Work any remaining pieces of glass back and forth until they're loose enough to pull out. Knock out any stubborn pieces with hammer.

2. Remove all old putty from frame, using chisel or scraper to pry it out. Look for fasteners that held glass in place—metal tabs called glaziers' points in wood-frame windows; spring clips in metal frames. If putty doesn't come out easily, apply linseed oil to it, and let oil soak in. Then scrape out softened putty, being careful not to gouge out window frame.

3. Apply linseed oil on raw wood around pane to prevent new putty from drying out too fast. If frame is metal, apply rust-resistant paint.

4. Measure frame for new glass. It should be just smaller than window opening to allow for expansion and contraction and to allow for imperfections in frame or glass. Measure both ways across opening, from inside edge to inside edge, and subtract $\frac{1}{16}$ to $\frac{1}{8}$ inch each way. Have double-strength glass cut to these precise dimensions. Purchase enough new glaziers' points or spring clips to be installed every 6 inches or so around pane.

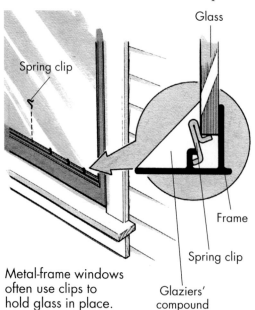

Glass

Spring clip

Frame

Spring clip

Glaziers' compound

Metal-frame windows often use clips to hold glass in place.

5. Install new glass using glaziers' compound or putty. Roll large chunk of compound between your palms to make long cord (about diameter of pencil). Starting at a corner, press compound into outside corner of window frame, where glass will rest. Cover entire perimeter of frame. With compound in place, carefully set new pane of glass into frame, pressing it firmly against compound. Press hard enough to flatten, squeezing out air bubbles and forcing out some of the compound around frame. Then, to hold glass in place, install new glaziers' points or spring clips every 6 inches or so around pane. Push points partway into wood with blade of putty knife held flat against glass; if the frame is metal, snap spring clips into holes in frame.

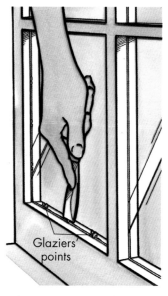

Glaziers' points

Glaziers' points hold the glass in place in a wood-frame window. Push the points in with a putty knife.

6. To seal new pane with glaziers' compound all around outside edge, roll another cord of glaziers' compound, and press it firmly into the glass-frame joint, all around pane. Use putty knife to smooth compound all along joint around pane, matching putty to other nearby windows. Hold putty knife at an angle to lip of frame, so knife cuts off compound cleanly and evenly along glass. If putty knife sticks or pulls at glaziers' compound, dip blade into linseed oil, and shake off excess. Use long, smooth strokes to keep joint even around pane.

7. With razor blade or glass scraper, carefully remove excess glaziers' compound from both sides of new glass and frame. Let compound dry for about three days.

8. Paint new compound and frame to match rest of frame. Lap paint slightly over edge of compound and onto glass to seal pane completely. Make sure paint is dry before you clean glass.

QUICK INTERIOR PAINTING TIPS

Painting can be a task that takes a couple of hours, a half day, or even longer. Whatever size job you decide to tackle, the painting techniques remain the same.

PREPPING FOR QUICK PAINTING

If you're painting over a previously painted surface, look for rough, peeling, or chipped areas. To find flaws, remove all the furniture from the room. Cluster the furniture in one area, and cover it and the floors with drop cloths. Take down the draperies and the drapery hardware. Loosen the light fixtures; let them hang and wrap them with plastic bags. Remove the wall plates from electrical outlets and switches. After fixing any flaws, wash down the surfaces to be painted with warm water and a good household detergent or wall-cleaning soap.

Don't attempt to paint over a surface that already has a glossy finish, even if it is clean. Glossy surfaces don't provide enough adhesion for new paint. To cut the gloss on an entire wall, wash it down with wall cleaner. Swab it on the wall, and sponge it dry. Rinse with clear water, then sponge dry again.

You can use deglossing solutions on woodwork too, or you can give woodwork a light sanding with medium- or fine-grade sandpaper. Wipe off or vacuum the resulting powder before you paint. On baseboards, remove accumulations of floor wax or acrylic floor finish with a wax remover or finish remover.

Scraping

The older your house, the greater the chance there's an area that needs scraping. A previous paint job may have begun to peel or crack in some places. Windowsills and sash frames may have chipped, or the old paint may have "alligatored" into a maze of cracks. If you find these conditions, scrape them gently to remove the loose particles, then sand them smooth to blend with the area around them. If you get down to bare wood on woodwork, prime the spots before you apply the final coat of paint. If it's impossible to blend the scraped areas with the nonscraped areas on walls, go over them with a light coat of drywall joint compound. When walls are dry, sand them smooth, prime, and paint.

Masking

Where two new paint colors come together on a single surface, it's practically impossible to keep a straight line between them while painting freehand with either a brush or a roller. To get a straight line, use a carpenters' level and a pencil to draw a faint line on the wall. Then, align masking tape with the line across the wall. Peel the tape off the roll a little at a time, and press it to the wall with your thumb. Don't pull the tape too tightly as you go, or it may stretch and retract once it's in place. To keep the paint from seeping under the masking tape, use the bowl of a spoon to press the tape tightly to the surface.

Tightly press masking tape to the surface using the bowl of a spoon.

Remove the tape before the paint is dry. If you wait too long, the paint may peel away from the surface. With latex paint, you only need to wait a half hour or so before peeling off the tape. With alkyds, two to three hours is enough.

Masking tape is useful for protecting trim around doors, windows, built-ins, baseboards, or bookshelves. When you're brushing or rolling new paint on the wall, you won't have to slow down or worry about sideswiping the trim.

PAINTING EQUIPMENT

The selection of painting tools was covered on pages 14–17. Once you have assembled the materials and completed the prep work, you're ready to resuscitate those old, drab walls with clean, new paint. Here are a few techniques that will ensure a neater job.

Brushes

The grip you use depends on the brush you've chosen. Trim and sash brushes with pencil handles are grasped much as you would a pencil, with the thumb and the first two fingers of the hand. With beaver-tail handles on larger brushes, you'll need a stronger grip because the brushes are wider and heavier. Hold the handle with the entire hand, letting the handle span the width of your palm as you would hold a tennis racket. This technique works best when you're painting large, flat surfaces.

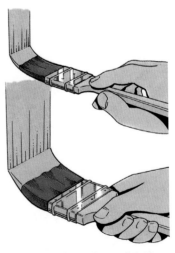

Grasp sash and trim brushes as you would a pencil (*top*). Hold a wall brush with your entire hand (*bottom*).

ESTIMATING PAINT JOBS

Estimating the paint you'll need for a job is easy. Take a few minutes at home to measure the area to be painted. Refer to the paint container for coverage information. A gallon of paint will typically cover about 400 square feet. If you're buying 2 or more gallons of the same color, it's a good idea to mix them all together at home so color variations don't show up in the middle of a wall.

To determine the amount of paint required to cover a wall, multiply the height of the wall by its length, then divide by 400. This means a gallon of paint will cover a 10×15-foot room (two 10-foot walls and two 15-foot walls, 8 feet high) with one coat. Two coats will take 2 gallons. However, there are other factors you should consider when calculating coverage.

When a wall is textured or rough-troweled, it will require more paint than if it were a smooth wall. For medium-rough, porous, or previously unpainted walls, you can safely estimate 300 to 350 square feet of coverage from a gallon of paint.

Most walls have doors or windows or other areas that are not painted. If the nonpainted area is a single window or door, ignore it in your calculations. Two or three windows, a door and a window, multiple sliding doors, or a fireplace reduce the paint you'll need. Multiply the lengths by the widths of these nonpaint areas to get the total square footage that you can subtract from your overall surface figures, or you can subtract about 15 square feet for typical windows and 21 square feet for typical doors. If you're painting the ceiling, figure its square foot area at width times length too.

Start the job by dampening the bristles of the brush (with water for latex or the appropriate thinner for other types of paint). Remove excess moisture by gently striking the metal band around the handle's base against the edge of your palm and into a sink or bucket.

With the first dip, move the brush around a bit in the paint to open the bristles and let the brush fill completely. It will be easier to pick up a full load if you jab the brush gently into the paint with each dip. With most latex paints, you can simply dip the brush and let the excess drip off for a few seconds before moving the brush to the wall. With thinner coatings, however, you may have to gently slap the brush against the inside of the paint can or lightly drag it across the inside edge of the lip to remove excess paint.

To neatly paint up to a line where two edges or colors meet, called "cutting in," use a trim brush with beveled bristles (the end of the brush resembles a chisel). Paint five or six strokes perpendicular to the edge of the ceiling or the wall. Next, smooth over these strokes with a single, long stroke, painting out from the corner first, then vertically. Where the wall and ceiling come together, use downward strokes on the wall first followed by smooth horizontal strokes. On the ceiling itself, cut in strokes toward the center of the room, away from the wall. Then paint a smooth horizontal stroke on the ceiling that follows the direction of the wall. Even if you're using the same color of paint on adjoining surfaces, follow this method of cutting in with 2-inch-wide borders rather than just plopping a loaded brush directly into a corner. This will prevent drips, sags, and runs.

Another cutting-in approach, beading, can practically eliminate the need to use masking tape to protect one painted area from another. Use a beveled trim brush with nice long bristles. Hold the brush so that your thumb is on one side of the metal ferrule and your fingers are on the other. Press the brush lightly against the surface, then, as you move the brush, add just enough pressure to make the bristles bend away from the direction of your brushstroke. Keep the brush about 1/16 inch away from the

To cut in at a corner, paint out from the corner for five or six strokes, then smooth over them with a single, long, smooth stroke.

other colored surface. The bent bristles and the pressure will release a fine bead of paint that will spread into the gap.

With both methods of cutting in, but especially when you're dealing with two colors, it's better to have a brush that's too dry than one that's too wet. Go slowly and cut in 4 or 5 inches at a time. It will seem tedious at first, but your speed and accuracy will improve with practice.

Rollers

As with brushes, moisten the roller first with water for latex paint or the appropriate thinner for other types of paint. Roll out the excess moisture on a piece of scrap lumber or on a paper grocery bag. Don't use newspaper because the roller may pick up the ink. Fill the well of the roller pan about half full, and set the roller into the middle of the well. Lift the roller and roll it down the slope of the pan, stopping just short

Be careful not to run the roller so rapidly that centrifugal force causes it to spray droplets of paint.

of the well. Do this two or three times to allow the paint to work into the roller. Then, dip the roller into the well once more, and roll it on the slope until the pile is well saturated. You'll know immediately when you've overloaded the roller. It will drip en route to the wall and have a tendency to slide and smear instead of roll across the surface.

The most effective method of painting with a roller is to paint 2- or 3-square-foot areas at a time. Roll the paint on in a zigzag pattern without lifting the roller from the wall, as if you're painting a large M, W, or backward N. Then,

With a roller, begin by making an *M*, a backward *N*, or a *W* pattern about 3 feet square. Always start with an upstroke so paint won't run down the wall. Next, fill in the pattern with crosswise strokes. You should be able to paint each 3-square-foot area with one dip of the roller.

still without lifting the roller, fill in the blanks of the letters with crosswise strokes. Finish the area with light strokes that start in the unpainted area and roll into the paint. At the end of the stroke, raise the roller slowly so it does not leave a mark. Go to the next unpainted area, and repeat the zigzag technique, ending it just below or next to the first painted patch. Finally, smooth the new application, and blend it into the previously finished area.

PAINTING WALLS

Paint an entire wall before taking a break so the painted portions won't lose their wet edges. Then stand back, scan the wall, and cover any missed spots or smears. If you're using an extension handle on your roller, you may find it more convenient to start at one high corner and go all the way across the room with a series of completed zigzag patterns. If you're right-handed, start on a wall's left-hand corner; if you're left-handed, start on a wall's right-hand corner.

PAINTING CEILINGS

When rolling paint on a ceiling, maintain a wet edge at all times to avoid creating lines and ridges. If you're using fast-drying paint, you may have to work faster than you anticipated and without taking a break. Both speed and ease can be achieved by using an extension handle so you can paint from the floor instead of from a stepladder. Many roller handles are made to accept a screw-in extension that you can buy at a paint store, but you may want to see if the threaded end of your broom or mop handle will work.

PAINTING TIGHT SPOTS

You probably won't have enough room to use the zigzag technique described earlier over and under windows and above doors and doorways. Instead, just roll the paint on horizontally. For areas that are narrower than the standard 7- or 9-inch roller, use a 4-inch roller or a paintbrush.

PAINTING WOODWORK

Whether you decide to paint the woodwork first or last, be sure to inspect it for defects and make the necessary repairs before you actually get down to painting. If you'll be painting over already-glossy woodwork, sand it lightly with sandpaper or steel wool first to help with adhesion. Or, give it a coat of deglosser.

Painting trim progresses more slowly than cutting in walls and ceilings, and there's more room for error. Following are some tips for painting the specific types of woodwork.

Trim, Baseboards, and Wainscoting

If you're using only one color and one finish on all surfaces, you may want to paint the trim as you come to it in the process of painting the walls. If you decide to paint the trim first, mask it off with masking tape or painter's tape when you paint the ceiling and walls.

Use the cutting-in technique discussed on pages 70–71 to paint the top of a baseboard. Then, using a painting shield or a thin piece of cardboard as a movable masker, cut in along the floor. After that, you can fill the unpainted space between with long brushstrokes. Paint only 2 or 3 feet of baseboard at a time. Examine the surface for drips, spatters, and overlapped edges, and clean them up immediately.

Painting wainscoting or paneling requires a similar approach. Cut in along the top and bottom edges where the wainscoting meets the wall and the floor, just as you did with the baseboard. Next, paint the indented panels and the molding around them. Paint tends to collect in the corners of these panels, so your brushstrokes should be toward the center of the panel. On the raised surfaces around and between panels, work from the top down, and use up-and-down strokes on the verticals, back-and-forth strokes on the horizontals.

Windows, Doors, and Shutters

Flush doors—those with smooth, flat surfaces—are easy to paint with either a brush or a roller, but doors with inset

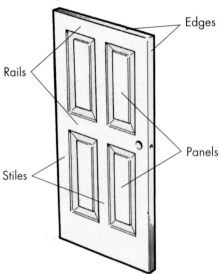

panels can be tricky. No matter what type of door you're dealing with, paint the entire door without stopping. Otherwise the lap marks may show. Before you start, remove the doorknobs, the plates behind them, and the latch plate on the edge of the door.

On ornate doors, start by painting the inset panels at the top of the door. As with wainscoting, paint all the panels and the molding around them. Then work your way down from the top to the bottom, painting the top rail, middle

When painting a door, paint the panels first. Then paint the rails, the stiles, and finally the edges, working from the top to the bottom.

Edges

Rails

Panels

Stiles

rail, and bottom rail (the horizontals) with back-and-forth strokes. Next, paint the vertical stiles (the sides) with up-and-down strokes. If you're painting both sides of the door, repeat this procedure. If you're painting only one side, paint the top edge of the door with a light coat. Over time, paint can build up on the top edge and cause the door to stick. Finally, paint the door's hinge edge and latch edge.

The job of painting windows will go faster if you purchase a 2- or 2½-inch sash trim brush, angled slightly across the bottom to make it easier to get into 90° corners and tight spaces.

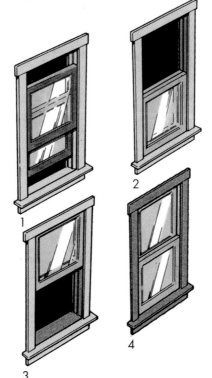

Paint double-hung windows in the sequence shown, moving the top and bottom sashes for access to all surfaces.

To paint wood-frame windows, first raise the bottom sash more than halfway up and lower the top sash until its bottom rail is several inches below the bottom sash. Paint the bottom rail of the top sash and up the stiles as far as you can go. Paint all the surfaces of the bottom sash except the top edge. Reverse the position of the sashes: top sash up to within an inch of the window frame, bottom sash down to within an inch of the windowsill. Then, paint the formerly obstructed surfaces of the top sash and the top edges of both sashes.

Don't paint the wood jambs in which the sashes move up and down yet. Instead, paint the window frame, working

PAINTING PRECAUTIONS

Except for the danger of falling off a ladder or scaffold, painting may not seem to pose much risk to the painter or other members of the family, but paint itself is a substance that can be hazardous to a person's health. Paint is a combination of chemicals and requires careful handling and proper precautions.

- Follow all safety precautions on the paint container.
- Water-thinned or solvent-thinned, paint ingredients are poisonous and should be kept away from children and pets. Antidotes are listed on can labels.
- Work in well-ventilated areas at all times, even if you're using odorless paints. They still contain fumes that may be harmful if inhaled. Wear a paper painters' mask when painting indoors. Also wear one outdoors if you're using an airless sprayer. Do not sleep in a room until the odor has dissipated.
- Do not smoke while painting and, if possible, extinguish pilot lights on gas appliances. Shut off gas to the unit first.
- Toxic paint chemicals can be absorbed through the skin. Wash up as soon as possible.
- When painting overhead, wear goggles to keep paint out of your eyes. Chemical ingredients can cause burns to sensitive eye tissue.
- Never drink alcohol while you're painting. Combined with paint fumes it can be deadly.

from top to bottom, including the sill. When the paint on the sashes is dry to the touch, move them both down as far as they will go. Paint the exposed jambs. Let the paint dry, raise both sashes all the way, and paint the lower jambs. To keep the sashes from sticking in the jambs, put on only as much paint as is necessary to cover the old coat. Wait for the paint to dry, then lubricate the channels with paraffin or a silicone spray.

The best way to paint shutters, both interior and exterior types, is to spray them, using either canned spray paint or an airless power sprayer. But you can still get a quality finish on old shutters by using a brush. Take them down and scrape, sand, and clean them as needed. Then, if you can hang them from an open ceiling joist—in the garage, for example—you can paint both sides at the same time. Otherwise, stand them upright or lay them out on the floor to paint one side at a time.

Keep your brush on the dry side. An excessively wet brush will result in runs and drips and, if the louvers are adjustable, sticking problems. Paint the window side of the shutter first. That way, if you do miss a run, it won't show. On adjustable shutters, put a wood matchstick or a little wood wedge between the adjusting rod and one or two of its staples to keep the rod away from the louvers. Paint the louvers first with a ½- or 1-inch trim brush. Then paint the frame with a 2-inch brush. Leave the shutter edges until last so you can periodically turn the shutter over to check for runs. If you find any, smooth them out with an almost-dry brush before they set. When the front is dry, paint the back.

CLEANING UP

One of the most important aspects of a successful paint job is keeping things clean as you're working. It's also important to clean equipment as soon as you're finished and to wipe up any spatters or drips as soon as they occur.

Minimizing Drips and Spatters

Even if you have already cut in around the room, avoid bumping the roller into the walls as you paint the ceiling or into the ceiling as you paint the walls. The roller may deposit a visible ridge of paint each time it touches the ceiling or the wall.

No matter how slowly and steadily you move the roller across a surface, it will emit a fine spray of paint. Wear a scarf or cap, and be sure the floor and furniture are covered with drop cloths.

If you choose not to mask around windows, doors, and woodwork, minimize the risk of spatters by using a paint shield. Store-bought shields come in several sizes and materials. Do-it-yourself shields can be made from thin cardboard or the slats of an old venetian blind. Holding the shield in one hand, place it perpendicular to the surface being painted. Then, with the other hand, apply the paint.

Because some spatters and spills are inevitable, keep a moist sponge and a pail of water handy when you're using latex paints. If you're using a solvent-thinned paint, keep some thinner and a supply of rags nearby to wipe up spatters and drips before they dry into bumps. Keep thinner and rags away from open flames as they are combustible.

Cleaning Windowpanes, Spatters, and Drips

The best time to clean up paint drips and spatters is when they're still wet and will wipe away easily. If you used masking tape around windows, peel it off right after painting. If

you painted freehand or with a painting shield, there will most likely be a few errant drops or smudges on the glass. A razor blade scraper will scrape the paint off the glass easily. Avoid breaking the seal between the new paint and the windowpane when you're cleaning up ragged edges around the sash.

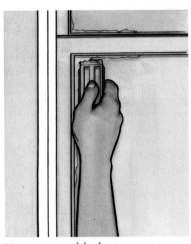

Use a razor blade scraper to remove dry paint from glass. Avoid breaking the seal between the paint and windowpane.

Cleaning up drips and spatters on most other surfaces is easier and less time consuming. For latex paint, a soft cloth with household detergent and warm water should do the trick. Don't scrub a freshly painted finish, though, even if it is dry to the touch. Many water-base paints don't cure for 30 days or more. For solvent-thinned paints, use a soft cloth and turpentine or mineral spirits to soften and remove dried-on paint droplets. Then, go over the area again with warm water and detergent.

To get paint drips off hardwood, ceramic tile, or resilient flooring, wrap a cloth around a putty knife and gently scrape them off. Then wash the areas with warm, soapy water. Don't use solvent if you can avoid it, as it can damage the finish on the floor.

Cleaning Painting Equipment

Fresh paint easily comes out of brushes, rollers, and pans; let paint dry for a while and you'll have to put a lot more time and effort into getting it out.

Inexpensive roller covers don't respond well even to thorough cleaning. Some paint residue will remain in the nap of the roller cover. When the roller is exposed to fresh paint later, the dried-in paint can soften and cause streaks in the new finish. If you use inexpensive roller covers, buy a new one for each job and save yourself the time and effort of trying to clean them. If you invest in a professional-quality roller cover, it will clean thoroughly and can be used repeatedly.

If you used latex paint, drag the brushes across the lip of the paint can to remove most of the paint. Then rinse the brushes and rollers under warm water and wash with dishwashing detergent. A paintbrush comb can help remove paint residue from the bristles. To get out the excess water, gently squeeze the bristles or take the brush outside and give it a few vigorous flicks. Squeeze the water out of the roller covers. Use paper towels to soak up any remaining water in both brushes and rollers.

With solvent-thinned paints, use the appropriate solvent as identified on the paint can's label. Agitate brushes and rollers in a container of the solvent. Repeat this process to get out all the paint. To clean brushes, pour the solvent into an old coffee can. For rollers, use an inexpensive aluminum foil loaf pan or a clean roller pan. Solvents are toxic and flammable, so don't smoke or work near a water heater or furnace, and be sure there's plenty of ventilation. Use paper towels to blot out the excess solvent from brushes and rollers, then wash everything in warm, soapy water. Hang up brushes until they're dry; set roller covers on end.

Wipe out, wash, and dry roller pans and paint containers. Wipe off the lips of paint cans and hammer down the lids to preserve leftover paint. Store paint and solvent cans away from extreme heat or cold and out of the reach of children. If you have less than a quart of paint left, store it in a tightly capped glass jar and save it for touch-ups. Brushes and rollers that have been cleaned and dried should be wrapped up before they're stored away. Brushes can go back in the plastic or paper packages they came in, or you can wrap them in aluminum foil. Rollers can be wrapped in kraft paper, foil, or perforated plastic sandwich bags.